BEING SOCIAL

Being Social

Ontology, Law, Politics

Edited by

Tara Mulqueen and Daniel Matthews

COUNTERPRESS
OXFORD

First published 2015
Counterpress, Oxford
http://counterpress.org.uk

© 2015 Tara Mulqueen and Daniel Matthews

Rights to publish and sell this book in print, electronic, and all other forms and media are exclusively licensed to Counterpress Limited. All other rights are reserved by the authors. An electronic version of this book is available under a Creative Commons Attribution-NonCommercial (CC-BY-NC 4.0) International license via the Counterpress website: http://counterpress.org.uk.

ISBN: 978-1-910761-00-7 (paperback)

Typeset in 10.5 on 12.5 pt Sabon

Cover by SUGAHTANK design
www.behance.net/SUGAHTANK

Global print and distribution by Ingram.

Contents

Introduction   1
DANIEL MATTHEWS AND TARA MULQUEEN

Part I Grounds of the Social   15

1   The Ground of Being Social   17
IAN JAMES

2   Being Social in 'Law and Society'   33
PETER FITZPATRICK

3   The Meaning of Sense   47
PIETER MEURS AND IGNAAS DEVISCH

Part II Acts of the Social   58

4   Being Social Democratically with Jean-Luc Nancy at the Gezi Park Protests   61
MARIE-EVE MORIN

5   The Queer Experience of Singular Finitude   76
TARA MULQUEEN

6   Labour and Migration in the 'Suspended Step'   90
ANASTASIA TATARYN

7   Survival's Witness: Poetry, Sociality, Community   101
PATRICK HANAFIN

8   On the Law of Originary Sociability or Writing the Law   114
DANIEL MATTHEWS

Index   129

Contributors

Ignaas Devisch is Professor of Philosophy and Ethics at Ghent University (Belgium). He publishes on social philosophy and the philosophy of medicine, and is the author of *Jean-Luc Nancy and the Question of Community* (Bloomsbury Press, 2012).

Peter Fitzpatrick is currently Anniversary Professor of Law at Birkbeck, University of London. He has taught at universities in Europe, North America, and Papua New Guinea and published books on legal philosophy, law and social theory, law and racism, and imperialism.

Patrick Hanafin is Professor of Law at Birkbeck, University of London, where he also directs the Law School's Centre for Law and the Humanities. His research engages with questions of law and the biopolitical, law and literature, human rights and citizenship, and the construction of community and identity. Of his many books, the most recent is, with Rosi Braidotti and Bolette Blaagaard, *After Cosmopolitanism* (Routledge, 2013).

Ian James is Reader in Modern French Literature and Thought at Downing College, University of Cambridge. He specialises in twentieth-century and contemporary French literature and philosophy. His many books include: *The Fragmentary Demand: An Introduction to the Philosophy of Jean-Luc Nancy* (Stanford University Press, 2006) and more recently, *The New French Philosophy* (Polity, 2012).

Daniel Matthews is Assistant Professor of Law at the University of Hong Kong. His primary research interests are in legal theory and law and literature. His current work assesses questions of jurisdiction, drawing on resources from law, literature and continental philosophy, with a particular focus on deconstruction. He is a member of the editorial committee of the journal *Law and Critique* and a regular contributor to *Critical Legal Thinking*, a blog dedicated to the radical critique of law and politics.

Pieter Meurs completed his PhD on Jean-Luc Nancy and globalization at the Centre Leo Apostel (Free University Brussels) in 2013. He has presented and published papers on phenomenology, critical theory, and Jean-Luc Nancy. His current research focuses on contemporary continental political philosophy.

Marie-Eve Morin is Associate Professor of Philosophy at the University of Alberta in Edmonton, Canada. Her research interests include phenomenology, existentialism, and deconstruction. She is the author of *Jean-Luc Nancy* (Polity Press, 2012), as well as articles on Heidegger, Sartre, Derrida, Nancy, and Sloterdijk. She is currently working on a comparative study of Nancy's and Merleau-Ponty's ontologies in light of the speculative realist challenge.

Tara Mulqueen is a doctoral candidate in law at Birkbeck, University of London. Her thesis concerns the creation of legislation for co-operatives in 19th century Britain, and the sources and significance of the particular form of recognition they received. In addition, she has researched and published on issues of gender and sexuality and social movements. She is also interested in questions of access to justice and community education.

Anastasia Tataryn teaches at Warwick Law School, University of Warwick and has previously taught at Birkbeck, University of London, where she is also completing her PhD. Drawing on legal theory and continental philosophy, her research focuses on labour and employment law, particularly with regards to precarious work in the UK and what it means to think differently about current political crises and legal grey areas.

Acknowledgements

We would like to thank Peter Fitzpatrick for raising the question and encouraging us to pursue the theme of 'being social.' Thanks to all of the contributors to the volume for their work and important insights, and to those who participated in the symposium and conference stream which fostered the ideas contained in these pages. We would also like to thank everyone at Counterpress for their guidance, intellectual camaraderie, and dedication in preparing the volume for publication.

Introduction

Daniel Matthews and Tara Mulqueen

> We exist as the anxiety of 'social Being' as such,
> where 'sociality' and 'society' are concepts
> plainly inadequate to its essence.
>
> — J.-L. Nancy[1]

Nearing the completion of this volume we somewhat worryingly found ourselves questioning the very premise of the project itself: being social. Our explorations of ontology, politics, and law in poststructural thought had appeared under this sobriquet in two seminars that gave rise to this collection but, as the project progressed, our title—though the words remained—appeared to change form, becoming strangely unfamiliar in our hands. Had 'the social,' a term at once ambiguous and overdetermined, really been our concern throughout? What had compelled us to labour under the title in the first place? And why this growing reticence with our chosen terminology? In many of its contemporary iterations the term 'social' has come to signify an unambiguous good. When used to qualify or supplement, for example, it denotes a heightened moral sensitivity, appearing in current vogue as social entrepreneurship or corporate social responsibility. Alternatively, 'being social,' in common parlance, could easily be taken to indicate an inclination or readiness to associate with others, to have non-abrasive characteristics, to be likeable, affable, or even pliant.

---

[1] Jean-Luc Nancy, Being Singular Plural, trans., Robert D Richardson and Anne E O'Byrne (Stanford : Stanford University Press, 2000), 43.

And more insidiously, the 'anti-social' are thought to present a threat to social cohesion and stability. Read in these terms, it might be assumed that this volume is a kind of vacuous self-help guide for the antisocial or socially awkward. This couldn't be further from our aim. That the title of the volume remains Being Social, however, perhaps promises too much: our anxieties persist. It is, as the opening lines from Nancy suggest, precisely an anxiety about the supposedly 'proper' delimitation of the social that our collective efforts here seek to address. Notwithstanding our diffidence, then, we concluded that it was a sense of the social that animates these pages but 'the social' in a form that challenges its common rendering.

The essays collected here speak to a sense of the social that resists final and precise determination, an uncanny and evanescent 'sociality' that, perhaps, reveals something of itself in its very obscurity. This elusive sociality, however, is not without political purchase. It is a key aim of this book to explore the politically engaged thinking and practices that might emerge from this re-worked account of being social. Our intervention responds to a common critique of poststructuralist thought: that it is unable to account for actual social relations and that it has little or nothing to contribute to political practice. It is often contended that poststructuralism, as a result of its disavowal of essence and truth, is unable to make any positive political or normative claims, fails to engage with material reality, and so confines itself to the textual or, at best, ethical realms. This critique, whilst rightly observing a suspicion with respect to essentialized modalities of identity and political positioning, misunderstands what is at stake in these concerns, on the one hand, and overlooks the opportunities for reconceiving sociality which emerge from deconstructve practices, on the other. This rather limited view of poststructural thought takes for granted the idea of the social which has been constructed and naturalized in late modernity. The assumed possibility of a positive normative truth claim, to which politics will inevitably have to answer, relies upon a preconceived sphere of activity in which meanings are given. The sense of the social to which these essays speak challenges this preconception, underscoring rather than effacing an anxiety of the social. With this collection, then, we do not seek to demonstrate how poststructuralist thought *is* social, but rather to explore how poststructuralist thought reconfigures sociality and how this reconfiguration effects thinking and practice in the legal and political realms.[2]

This reconfiguration is perhaps only the most recent in a long history of such transformations of being social. In antiquity, the social made reference to the sphere of the family and the pre-political meeting of physical and material necessities. As Hannah Arendt explains, for both Plato and Aristotle, sociality was something that was shared with animals, and not a uniquely human characteristic: 'the natural, merely social companionship of the human species was considered to be a limitation imposed upon us by the needs of biological life, which are the same for the human animal as for other forms of animal life.'[3] The rise of the Greek city-state created a second realm, a political and public order, which depended upon but superseded the social. As Arendt charts, a later elision between the social and the political collapsed these two previously distinct registers. In particular, Aquinas's comparison between the rule of the household and with political rule, betrayed a misunderstanding of the nature of the social in Greek thought.[4]

The concept of the social which emerges in modernity continues this elision, obscuring distinctions between public and private, and confusing what had been distinct political and social realms.[5] Significantly, these changes involve the re-imagination of the household as a paradigm of national governance: 'we see the body of peoples and political communities in the image of a family whose everyday affairs have to be taken care of by a

---

[2] As is well known, the question of politics in poststructural thinking is often thought through a meditation on the difference between politics (la politique) and the political (le politique). The former referring to the realm of decision and position, the latter to the ontological clearing or ground in which politics takes place. In the 1980s, Nancy and Lacoue-Labarthe pursued a re-thinking or 'retreatment' of the political, highlighting how the day-to-day life of politics obscures a prior register of the political. Changing the form of one's politics, it is suggested, must come with a retreatment of the political, a re-engagement with the grounds that are often obscured by the to and fro of action and decision. In what follows, we do not offer a detailed engagement with the politics/political difference. However, one might read the essays here as reasserting the idea that this very difference (of the politics/political) must always be thought together, persisting in a différantial relation. Though preference, context, or strategy might dictate that one term is temporally emphasized over the over, we suggest that politics always engages both registers, holding the ground of the political as a question at the very moment that one engages or decides in the register of politics.

[3] Hannah Arendt, *The Human Condition* (Chicago: The University of Chicago Press, 1958), 24.

[4] Arendt, *Human Condition*, 27.   [5] Arendt, *Human Condition*, 27.

gigantic, nation-wide administration of housekeeping.'⁶ With this shift the nation becomes cast as 'one super-human family ... call[ed] "society".'⁷ This expansion of the social has the consequence of eclipsing both the realms of family and of politics. It is concerned with conformity and a scientific conception of *behaviour*. In this process, man becomes a properly 'social being' and, through the science of economics, their behaviour can be analysed in relation to conformist standards which allow for the management of a 'normalized' sociality, and 'those who did not keep the rules could be considered to be asocial or abnormal.'⁸

In keeping with this, the turn of the nineteenth century saw the emergence of the so-called 'social body,' appearing alongside the expanding discourse of pauperism. More than mere poverty, which was defined largely as an economic problem, pauperism was a moral concern. As Poovey describes, 'the gradual consolidation of a distinctively "social" domain was facilitated by efforts to comprehend—to understand, measure, and represent—the poverty that seemed increasingly visible in the last three decades of the eighteenth century.'⁹ It is during the nineteenth century, as Karl Polanyi suggests, that the vision of men shifted 'toward their own collective being as if they had overlooked its presence before. A world was uncovered, the very existence of which had not been previously suspected, that of the laws governing a complex society.'¹⁰ Although this society was constructed from developments in economic thought, political economy extended it to a universal meaning. The problem of pauperism in society caused a great deal of anxiety about man and his community, accompanied by a vision

---

⁶ Arendt, *Human Condition*, 28–9. Since the financial crash of 2008 it is worth noting the way in which UK national debt is presented as analogous with a 'national credit card,' as if the result of irresponsible management of the household expenses.

⁷ Arendt, Human Condition, 28–9.

⁸ Arendt, Human Condition, 41–2. This is the conception of the social which becomes the object of social sciences. On this point, see Maus: 'Social phenomena were assumed to be subject like other phenomena to observable uniformities which can be studied, compared, and classified; in other words, social phenomena can be expressed by laws. Later on sociology was, rightly or wrongly, to do its best to comply with this demand and some writers even went so far as to insist that could be regarded as a science only to the extent to which it actually did so.' (Heinz Maus, *A Short History of Sociology* (London: Routledge, 1962), 5.)

⁹ Mary Poovey, *The Making of a Social Body: British Cultural Formation*, 1830–1864 (Chicago: University of Chicago Press, 1995), 8.

¹⁰ Karl Polanyi, *The Great Transformation: The Political and Economic Origins of Our Time* (Boston: Beacon Press, 2001 [1944]), 88.

of the perfectibility of that society. This vision motivated the social and philosophical theories of positivism and utilitarianism that dominated political and legal thought throughout the nineteenth century.

In *Society Must Be Defended*, Foucault provides a different but compatible account of the discovery or invention of modern society, placing its birth at the turn of the seventeenth century. This is 'a society whose historical consciousness centres not on sovereignty and the problem of its foundation, but on revolution, its promises, and its prophecies of future emancipation.'[11] For Foucault, this discourse of society was ambiguous: it could be taken up in the name of a variety of causes, from resistance to the justification of absolute monarchy to popular movements and in the discourse of 'racist biologists and eugenicists.'[12] The pervasive acceptance and naturalization of this conception of the social is demonstrated by its presence in thinkers as diverse as Malthus and Marx, who operated within a shared discourse, one which is predicated on a notion of economic society, and in which truth claims are made and validated through binary and oppositional structures. As an example of this continuity, we find Foucault quoting Marx, writing in a late letter to Engels: 'you know very well where we found our idea of class struggle; we found it in the work of the French historians who talked about the race struggle.'[13] These discourses and structures persist in various forms today and in turn shape our sense of the social, with its universal reference; as Polanyi suggests, 'our social consciousness [is] cast in ... [the] mould [of] society.'[14] The very way in which we conceive of the category of 'the social' is bound up in this conception of society, which, crucially, continues to structure how we conceptualize social change and the tenor and form of political practice.

The refiguring of the social within poststructuralist thought responds to this reification of the social which occurs in modernity. However, it is not an attempt to return to the idea of the social which was present in antiquity, to relegate it to the biological sphere and reinstate a rigid separation between the social and the political realms. Instead, the social of poststructuralist thought, variously

---

[11] Michel Foucault, *Society Must Be Defended* (London: Penguin Books, 2004), 80.
[12] Foucault, *Society*, 49–50.   [13] Foucault, *Society*, 79.
[14] Polanyi, *Great Transformation*, 87–8.

articulated as 'sociality,' 'sociability,' or 'community' attempts to re-imagine it in an explicitly ontological mode. There are more or less significant differences amongst poststructuralist theorists as to the status of this sociality; the notion of the social informing the present essays takes it to be the condition of possibility for determination and signification as such. In this sense, the social must be read as a problem—perhaps even *the* problem—of being. With its focus on the ontological, then, *Being Social* seeks to return the first questions of philosophy to the experience of a social life, common to all: of friends passed and strangers to come, of loved ones as much as the figure of the whomever (or whatever) with whom any 'I' is always already in relation.[15] In this sense, the 'being social' of our title speaks both to an abstract or philosophical register and a material or sensual one. Through Jean-Luc Nancy in particular, we claim that the question of being must be articulated as a matter of both plurality (being for us is always a matter of being-with or *Mitsein*) and materiality, praxis and action. As Meurs and Devisch make clear in their elaboration of Nancy's thinking of 'sense' in the present volume, being must be understood as something *active* and *creative*, an on-going fashioning of being-in-the-world.[16] In this sense, the formulation of ontology that undergirds the essays collected here seeks to fold the ontological register within the worldly and experiential, to the on-going, sensed, and practical questions, actions, and creativity of lives lived with others. With this move we are following a vein in poststructural thought that casts sociality as the excess which maintains the constitutive openness and contingency of representation, rather than a pre-determined entity or essence; but we want to stress that this excess is immanent to a sensed, material, and creative (social) life.

In Derrida's formulation we might read this primary register of the social as the 'law of originary sociability ... the very essence of law.'[17] Or for Blanchot, it might be found in the 'unavowable com-

---

[15] As James notes in his chapter in the present collection this 'with' must also involve the non-human world.

[16] See p. 56. This creative imperative directly challenges orthodox accounts of globalization, suggesting an alternative mode of world-creation or world-forming that resists the hegemonic construction of a supposedly 'globalized' world. See also Jean-Luc Nancy, *The Creation of the World; Or Globalization*, trans. François Raffoul and David Pettigrew (New York: State University of New York Press, 2007).

[17] Jacques Derrida, *Politics of Friendship*, trans., George Collins (London: Verso, 2005), 231.

munity,' that seeks to capture a sense of 'a world which is ours for being nobody's.'[18] For Nancy, whose thinking is perhaps the most significant for the present collection, sociality emerges through a meditation on the *inoperative community* and *being with*, the fact that we are always-already in common, in an 'originary or ontological "sociality."'[19] This sociality is introduced by contrasting it with the modern notion of society. Citing Rousseau, Nancy characterizes 'society' as a manifestation of a longing for a lost community, in a way that is very similar to Polanyi and others quoted earlier.[20] He warns us that we must be suspicious of this notion of society, which 'means questioning the breakdown in community that supposedly engendered the modern era.'[21] For Nancy, the sense of longing which could be said to undergird conceptions of society is misplaced, if not completely illusory, because '*community has not taken place*, or rather, if it is indeed certain that humanity has known (or still knows, outside of the industrial world) social ties quite different from those familiar to us, community has never taken place along the lines of our projections of it according to these different social forms.'[22] Moreover, he claims that:

> Society was not built on the ruins of a *community*. It emerged from the disappearance or the conservation of something—tribes or empires—perhaps just as unrelated to what we call 'community' as to what we call 'society.' So that community, far from being what society has crushed or lost, is *what happens to us*—question, waiting, event, imperative—*in the wake of society*.[23]

We follow Nancy here in claiming that none of these conceptions of social relation—whether society, tribe or empire—corresponds to community. Community simply *is*, as a condition of our existence, prior to all of these formulations or appropriations of that relationality.

But does this assertion of an ontological, and thus inescapable, plane of sociality not return us to the 'grounds' or 'foundations'

---

[18] Maurice Blanchot, *The Unavowable Community*, trans., Pierre Jorris (New York: Station Hill, 1988), 29.

[19] Jean-Luc Nancy, *The Inoperative Community*, trans., Peter Connor, Lisa Garbus, Michael Holland, and Simona Sawhney (Minneapolis: University of Minnesota, 2003), 28.

[20] Nancy, *Inoperative*, 10.   [21] Nancy, *Inoperative*, 9.   [22] Nancy, *Inoperative*, 11.

[23] Nancy, *Inoperative*, 11.

which characterize prior conceptions of the social? Are we not repeating the very gesture that we purportedly seek to supersede in this collection? To be clear, our distrust of ultimate foundations does not efface the figure of the 'ground' or 'foundation' entirely. To assert the absolute groundlessness of being social either leads to an abyssal and dangerous nihilism or returns us, by way of a kind of negative theology, to the very 'ground' which such an approach purports to be without. The 'post-foundational' mode to which the essays here speak retains a thinking of grounds, essences, and so on, but transforms their sense, resisting the assertion of a sovereign, natural, or immutable foundation from which thinking might proceed.[24] This move 'implies an increased awareness of ... contingency' and the multiplicity of partial and always already compromised grounds.[25] In our account, the social as 'ground' then, defies the onto-theology of metaphysics. It is a 'ground' that always already conditions the possibility of things but is itself elusive, withdrawing at the very moment it is claimed or delimited.[26] Such a re-working of the ground involves a thinking that is neither strictly immanent nor transcendent. The transcendent ground—typically associated with a classical account of sovereignty—is eschewed but so too is an all-encompassing immanentism that offers no access to a *beyond* of the purely present or given. Significantly, the 'trans-immanence' of being social affirms the opening of possibilities to come (*à venir*), beyond a given arrangement, at the very same time it suggests that such an opening to transcendence is immanent to the material, bodily, and sensed experience of world.[27]

This collection explores this doubled sense of 'being social,' examining how thinking of ontology as being co-extensive with a sense of the social informs scholarship and everyday practice. Such thinking requires a re-working of categories in both 'legal'

---

[24] The term 'post-foundational' was coined by Oliver Marchart in his excellent book which seeks to address the complex appropriation and re-thinking of grounds in much contemporary thought; see Oliver Marchart, *Post-Foundational Political Thought: Political Difference in Nancy, Lefort, Badiou and Laclau* (Edinburgh: Edinburgh University Press).

[25] Marchart, *Post-Foundational*, 2.

[26] Ian James's essay in the present volume provides a rich account of this re-thinking of the 'ground' of the social.

[27] Derrida makes a key distinction between the future—conceived as a recasting of the present, thought in terms of the present, a 'future present'—and the 'to come' (*à venir*) which is associated with the event, signalling an alternative temporality beyond presence.

and 'political' traditions. And so too do the terms and categories that animate politics change form. In Nancy's terms, democracy does not simply name one political regime or mode of political engagement amongst others. Nancy's democracy—an account crucial for Morin's contribution here—is an originary sharing out of being that makes possible the constitution of the political itself. Echoing Derrida's claim that 'the democracy to come would be like the *khora* of the political,'[28] we might call this 'truth' to democracy *arche*-political, describing an originary sense of being social which must be presupposed for politics proper to take place. In more general terms, the post-foundational account of 'being social' re-invigorates the social bond, negotiating a path, as Morin puts it, between 'totalilization and atomization.'[29] In this sense, the necessary coincidence of self and other reasserts the significance of social and communal bonds and obligations but disavows their supposed stability.

It is with reference to the *bonds* and *obligations* associated with 'being social' that we can sense the importance of re-thinking legal as well as political categories, and with that address a preoccupation in this volume with questions of law. As with our re-thinking of the social, we want to pursue a sense of the law that takes on an ontological register. Let us return to Heidegger's *Geworfenheit* or 'throwness' of being in order to reflect a little on the changing form of the legal as well as political bonds that we seek to explore in these essays. Nancy re-imagines *Geworfenheit* in terms of 'abandonment' and in so doing inscribes a legal category into the heart of being. Etymologically, abandonment is rooted in *bandon* meaning 'jurisdiction, license and control.' Abandonment, as well as referring to the general condition of 'groundless' and 'throwness' also means being cast beyond a particular jurisdiction, banished from the authority of law. However, Nancy insists that to be abandoned (which, following Heidegger, must be thought as the very 'essence' of being) is not to be removed from law entirely. Rather, he suggests, 'one always abandons *to* a law,'[30] rather than being simply banished *from* a particular set of laws within a jurisdiction. This law to

---

[28] Jacques Derrida, *Rogues: Two Essays on Reason*, (Stanford: Stanford University Press, 2004), 82.
[29] See p. 66.
[30] Jean-Luc Nancy, *The Birth to Presence*, trans., Brian Holmes et al (Stanford: Stanford University Press, 1993), 44.

which we are abandoned is a law of an un-worked trans-immanent sociality, a law of restless connection by which we are bound but in a way that resists ossification. In Nancy's pithy formulation this involves the tying of the '(k)not,' at once suggesting a bond created and secured but one that is always already negated, a ligament undone in its tying.[31]

The essays here that engage law often do so in these terms. We are, Nancy stresses, abandoned at birth and so are forced or compelled to be in a state of abandonment. This is 'the other of the law' that precedes juridical law and is revealed through a withdrawal of fixity or determinacy.[32] In Nancy's formulation, abandonment from the law does not mean that we are abandoned to a particular place or space beyond the law; rather, abandonment means being cast beyond such particularities. There is abandonment—and this is the law.

Perhaps here we are returned to the anxiety with which we opened this introduction. If the law (of abandonment) becomes akin to the social itself, we are left with the task, as Peter Fitzpatrick points out,

> of saying what is distinct about this law setting it apart from, as well as remaining of, society—a law that is not ultimately subsumed within or ultimately 'explained' by society empirically encased; a law that embeds possibility yet still ranges beyond it.[33]

Following Fitzpatrick, let us conclude, then, by affirming that this law of the social must be thought in terms other than a metaphysics of presence. The sociality evoked in this book is very much *here*, at play within this very 'present' moment, but at the very same time, its sense is always deferred, pointing elsewhere and 'ranging beyond' the claims of presence or stability. As we have tried to stress in this introduction, this does not mean that the social is forever postponed, always transcending the *hic et nunc*; rather, its elusiveness and its temporal alterity must be thought as being walled up within the very 'presence' that it exceeds. This opening to the 'to come' will always imply both a threat and a promise. The sense of the social that resists a final determination allows for the

---

[31] Jean-Luc Nancy, *The Sense of the World*, trans., Jeffrey S Librett (Minneapolis: University of Minnesota, 1997), 92–3.
[32] Nancy, *Finite Thinking*, 44.
[33] See p. 45.

coming of the event, of political praxis and action that transforms the current arrangement of things. But the inoperativity of the social means that there can be no guarantee of the righteousness of one's actions. This perhaps explains the persistence of our anxiety of the social—to think of the social in the terms discussed in this book is to be exposed to a trembling of grounds and a fraying of fixed frames of reference that puts all of us, and our sociality itself, in question. Perhaps, in the end, we might find some quiet solace in this common anxiety of social being.

∽

LET US CONCLUDE by briefly outlining the contributions and foregrounding a couple of themes and concerns. Firstly, amongst all the references in the pages that follow, from Butler to Blanchot, Foucault to Laruelle, readers will note that one name looms larger than others. The fact that Jean-Luc Nancy is given such prominence is not the result of editorial direction, rather it simply testifies to the richness of his thinking on the questions that preoccupy us here. Amongst all those contemporary thinkers who are following and re-working deconstructive themes and practices (Catherine Malabou, Bernard Stiegler, Judith Butler, *et al*), Nancy's work is exceptional in that it develops a philosophically sophisticated account of the inescapable and primary fact of social life. Nancy's work addresses a diverse set of philosophical questions: ontological, bodily and material, aesthetic, and political.[34] Since the 1980s, Nancy—along with his co-conspirator, Philippe Lacoue-Labarthe—has figured prominently in debates around community and the nature of 'the political.' But his more recent work on the ontology of 'being singular plural'[35] and 'sense'[36] is now informing many interventions in legal and political scholarship.[37] The essays here

---

[34] For an introduction to Nancy's thought, see Ian James, *The Fragmentary Demand: An Introduction to the Philosophy of Jean-Luc Nancy* (Stanford: Stanford University Press, 2006) and Marie-Eve Morin, *Jean-Luc Nancy* (New York: Wiley, 2012)

[35] See Nancy, *Being Singular Plural*.   [36] See Nancy, *Sense of the World*.

[37] Recent publications include Benjamin Hutchens ed., *Jean-Luc Nancy: Justice, Legality and World* (London: Continuum, 2012); Illan rua Wall, *Human Rights and Constituent Power: Without Model or Warranty* (Oxford: Routledge, 2011); Peter Gratton and Marie-Eve Morin eds., *Jean-Luc Nancy and Plural Thinking* (New York: SUNY Press, 2012); and Gilbert Leung, *Jean-Luc Nancy: The First Question of Law* (forthcoming).

follow, in part at least, this endeavour to address a wide range of Nancy's thinking, particularly stressing Nancy's account of 'trans-immanence' that underpins his more recent work.

The opening section—*'grounds' of the social*—outlines the contours of a poststructural account of the social and its complex implication with law and politics. Throughout, our focus is the *sense* of the social and this thinking of 'sense' is given a technical elaboration in Pieter Meurs and Ignaas Devisch's contribution. An understanding of 'sense' is developed that both precedes and exceeds signification. This thinking is crucial to the account of sociality that underpins the essays collected here: our task is at once to *make sense* of the social and to allow the social to appear *as sense*. At this juncture we can note that such an aspiration—to 'make sense of the social'—necessarily entails an aporetic encounter with a self-legislative logic. As Ian James argues, any claim to delimit the nature of the social within a given discourse or discipline involves a claim that that particular perspective has the right to 'legislate for, and therefore to determine' the essence of the 'human' and the 'social.'[38] In this sense, an account of the social necessarily infers certain *legal* pre-determinations. Such an attention to the law's relation to the social is explored in Peter Fitzpatrick's contribution. Here he accounts for the legal dimension to both theorizing and providing content for the social by arguing that we must position law as an ambivalent and constitutively fragile mechanism by which the social can be brought into a determinative and delimited form. This mechanism, however, is always already exceeding itself, opening both the law and the social to new possibilities to come.

The intersection between the social, political, and legal is drawn out in all eight pieces of this volume, with a particular focus on how a re-imagination of the social, at a theoretical register, must be pursued alongside a re-invigoration of forms of political action. The latter mode is the focus of the second section—*acts of the social*.[39] Here the essays explore the ways in which a poststructural

---

[38] See p. 17.

[39] An 'act' refers to some action, deed or performance for which someone (some actor) might be held responsible. To 'act' also evokes performance in the sense of pretence and might be used to describe simulation, theatrical representation as well as activities of counterfeiting or fakery. An 'Act,' too, is some decree or edict issued from a legislative body. The essays in the 'acts of the social' section engage all of these senses of 'act' and 'acting,' examining questions of praxis, performativity, and pretence as well as those associated with law and the institutions of government.

thinking of the social is refracted through a series of political and legal practices and concerns. Tara Mulqueen's engagement with Blanchot and Nancy in the context of the queer politics of the 1980s and 90s and Marie-Eve Morin's assessment of Nancy's account of democracy in relation to forms of resistance in the Istanbul uprisings of 2013, both illustrate that the ontological question of the social cannot be separated from modes of political practice. For Patrick Hanafin, Daniel Matthews, and Anastasia Tataryn, practices of 'writing' (though variously understood through the poetry of Guantanamo, the on-going play between 'inscription/exscription,' or as 'literary communism') offer a means through which we might account for 'an inoperative living-with legality.'[40] Though clearly influenced by a Derridean sense of 'writing' (or *écriture*), Hanafin, Matthews, and Tataryn reveal another aspect to writing by exploring—through Nancy in particular—the way in which a differed and deferred sense of the social itself takes a writerly form.

---

[40] See p. 109.

Grounds
of the
Social

— 1 —

The Ground of Being Social

Ian James

Foundations, the Human, Sociability

The ability of philosophy to account for human sociability appears to be necessarily bound up with the specific images of human nature or essence that philosophy proposes or presupposes. This ability also appears, perhaps decisively, to be bound up with the right that philosophy claims for itself to legislate for, and therefore to determine, such images of human nature or essence. If this is so, then for philosophy to describe or prescribe a ground for our social being it must, in turn, be secure in the foundational image of the human it presupposes, and secure also in the philosophical foundations which will allow it, *as philosophy*, to secure such an image of the human.

There are a number of foundational moments in modern philosophy when this interplay between the understanding of human sociability, its grounding in human nature, and philosophy's powers of self-legislation and self-grounding can be discerned. So, for instance, in Hume's *Treatise on Human Nature* the capacity for sympathy emerges as the fundamental framework around which a philosophical understanding of social relations and what might be termed a 'sociology of human nature' is developed.[1] For Hume, the ability to sympathize with others, and to enter into diverse

---

[1] Christopher J. Finley, *Hume's Social Philosophy* (London: Continuum, 2007), 105.

modes of relation and communication with them is one of the most fundamental characteristics of being human and underpins a variety of emotion and behaviour: 'No quality in human nature,' he writes, 'is more remarkable [...] than that propensity we have to sympathize with others, and to receive by communication their inclination and sentiments.'[2] Moreover, this capacity for sympathy is predicated upon, and is heightened in proportion with, the experience of similarity or resemblance. Hume writes: 'where [...] there is any peculiar similarity in our manners, or character, or country, or language, it facilitates sympathy.'[3] As Christopher Finlay has highlighted, sympathy, in Hume's *Treatise*, is based on the association of ideas and feelings and their perceived resemblance *in experience*.[4]

So Hume's view of human nature ('wherein the force of sympathy is very remarkable'[5]) provides the basis for his account of human sociability and both find their ground in his empirical method and the theory of simple ideas and impressions in which that method is itself grounded. This is clear from the way in which Hume asserts that sympathy and its relation to sociality are observable and evident in experience rather than being the product of purely philosophical theorizing. It is also clear in the way that he understands sympathy in terms of the experience of impressions and ideas of others formed through association and resemblance:

> 'Tis indeed evident, that when we sympathize with the passions of others, these movements appear at first in *our* mind as mere ideas, and are conceived to belong to another person .... 'Tis also evident, that the ideas of the affections of others are converted into the very impressions they represent, and that the passions arise in conformity to the images we form of them. All this is an object of the plainest experience, and depends not on any hypothesis of philosophy.[6]

So here the theory of sympathy as the basis of sociability is empirically grounded insofar as it is observable as an experiential evidence. Moreover, it is at the very same time constructed out of the terms which ground the empirical method itself, that is to

---

[2] David Hume, *A Treatise on Human Nature*, ed. L. A. Selby-Bigge (Oxford: Clarendon Press, 1888), 316 [II.I.XI].
[3] Hume, *Treatise on Human Nature*, 318 [II.I.XI].
[4] Finlay, *Hume's Social Philosophy*, 110.
[5] Hume, *Treatise on Human Nature*, 363 [II.II.V].
[6] Hume, *Treatise on Human Nature*, 319–20 [II.I.XI].

say the Humean account of ideas and impressions, images and passions which, the *Treatise* tells us, are the very stuff or evidence of experience itself.[7] In the *Treatise* philosophy legislates for its own foundation or ground in the sole appeal to experience, to impressions and ideas as the very *stuff* of experience. It then offers an image of the human, of human sympathy and sociability which it similarly grounds in observable self-evident elements of experience. These moments, when taken together, form a consistent, interrelated, and interdependent whole.

A similar consistency, interrelatedness or interdependence of moments can be discerned in the account of sociability proposed in that other foundational moment of modern philosophy, Kantian critique. This is particularly evident in the account of aesthetic judgment and of taste that Kant gives in the *Critique of Judgment*. In the third *Critique*, Kant explicitly links notions of human nature, sociability, and the communicability of judgments of taste:

> If we admit the impulse to society as natural to man, and his fitness for it, and his propension towards it, *i.e. sociability*, as a requisite for man being destined to society, and so as a property belonging to *humanity*, we cannot escape from regarding taste as a faculty for judging everything in respect of which we can communicate our feeling to all other men.[8]

So Kant's image of the human poses sociability as a natural property which destines us to society and which at the very same time *necessarily* determines taste as a faculty of judgment which exists in relation to the possibility of universal social communication ('*all other men*' [my emphasis]). Kant goes onto note that the aesthetic pleasure we might take in objects of taste may be considerable but that 'the idea of its universal communicability increases its worth in an almost infinite degree.'[9] So here the image of human nature as innately social and the possibility of universal communication of judgments of taste appear as intimately bound up each with the other. Just as, in Hume, the elements of human sociability, sympathy, found their ground and consistency in the empirical method and in the theory of ideas and impressions in which that

---

[7] Hume, *Treatise on Human Nature*, 4 [I. I. I.].
[8] Immanuel Kant, *The Critique of Judgment* (New York: Cosimo, 2007), 104.
[9] Kant, *Critique of Judgment*, 104.

method was itself grounded, so, in Kant, sociability, judgments of taste, and universal communicability all form parts of a consistent interlinking whole which is itself grounded in a broader conception of human autonomy, freedom, and reason which underpins the unity and coherence of all three of the *Critiques*. Kant expresses this in terms which both resonate with, but also diverge from, those of Hume:

> *Humanity* on the one side indicates the universal *feeling of sympathy*, and on the other the faculty of being able to *communicate* universally our inmost feelings. For these properties taken together constitute the characteristic social spirit of humanity by which it is distinguished from the limitations of animal life.[10]

Like Hume, Kant identifies the feeling of sympathy as an essential aspect of human nature which underpins our social being but, rather than relating sympathy to empirical observation, to impressions, passions, and the ideas we have of them, he more immediately relates it to our capacity for universalization and therefore to human freedom and to the a priori conditions of experience determined as both universal and necessary. For both Hume and Kant sympathy, that is, the communicability of feelings, emotions or judgments, provides a ground for sociability with such communicability itself being grounded in the experience of resemblance on the one hand and the capacity for universalization on the other. In each case the image of the human and the account of human social being find their basis in the broader philosophical ground that the philosophical system legislates for itself, the empirical and transcendental-critical method respectively.

The Withdrawal of Foundation and Ground

To highlight this interdependence, in Kant and Hume, of philosophy's understanding of the human, its account of human social being, and the ground or foundation that philosophy legislates for itself, is perhaps to remark on the obvious, namely that both are offering a system of thought which aims to give a *total* image of the human and of the conditions (empirical or transcendental) for *all* human experience. The very consistency or coherence of

[10] Kant, *Critique of Judgment*, 151.

the system may be, very precisely, what guarantees philosophy's authority. Indeed, a contemporary thinker such as François Laruelle has argued that it is in the very nature or essence of philosophy to offer a totalizing image, conceptual system, or discourse on reality and on human being.[11] According to Laruelle, philosophy, that is to say, *all* philosophy (of whatever kind, e.g. empiricist, idealist, logical, analytical, phenomenological, existential, deconstructive, etc.) aims to synthesize the totality of the real into a system of concepts or discursive operations and does so by making fundamental legislative decisions as to what the ground of the real may be. Yet, Laruelle also argues, philosophy's founding decisions, or indeed what he calls the *philosophical decision* as such, lead it always into a circularity of thought. A philosophy starts from a specific originary decision (for example, a decision in favour of empirical evidence or transcendental universality and necessity) and develops insights and conclusions which then justify that initial decision by dint of their consistency with it. That the originary assumption or decision may be ultimately arbitrary is what renders the circularity achieved by philosophical consistency perhaps more vicious than virtuous.[12]

If one were to follow Laruelle and call into question the basis or ground of the philosophical decision, that is to say, the basis or ground upon which philosophy legislates for its own systematic power to truth, then the power of thought to offer an account of human social being and indeed, its power to offer an image of human being per se, are also radically called into question. The interdependence of terms and consistency of thought that was exemplified in the systems of Kant and Hume, shows that, without a philosophical ground or foundation the determination of a universal image of the human, and therefore of human sociality, may be impossible. Without an ability to legislate for its own ground and universal power, philosophy cannot legislate for or determine an image of human nature, and cannot, therefore, have any competency in offering a general view of human sociability.

---

[11] See François Laruelle, *Philosophy and Non-philosophy*, trans. Taylor Adkins (Minneapolis: Univocal, 2013); François Laruelle, *Principles of Non-philosophy*, trans. Nicola Rubczak & Anthony Paul Smith (London: Bloomsbury, 2013).
[12] On what Laruelle calls the *Principle of Sufficient* Philosophy (*PSP*), see Laruelle, *Philosophy and Non-Philosophy*, 12–13; on the circularity of the philosophical decision, see Ian James, *The New French Philosophy* (Cambridge: Polity, 2012), 164–6.

Jean-Luc Nancy is a contemporary thinker who, like Laruelle, has placed the critique of philosophy's foundational gestures at the very centre of his thinking. Like Laruelle, he radically calls into question the power of philosophy to legislate for its own capacity to determine its foundations and therefore to give an image of, or lay a universal ground for, the human. Unlike Laruelle, however, Nancy's critique of philosophy's (self-)foundation is intimately tied up with a renewed thinking of sociality or of social being. Thinking at the limits of philosophical discursiveness, and in the radical absence of any philosophical foundation, Nancy also, and necessarily, thinks in the absence of any determinate image of the human but this does not prevent him from developing an understanding of social being or for thinking the specific modality of being social in the most fundamental terms.

Abyss, Freedom, Relation

Nancy's work of the 1970s and early 1980s, most notably the essays devoted to Kant in *Logodaedalus: Discours de la syncope* (1976) and *L'Impératif catégorique* (1983), develops this critique of philosophical foundations through meticulous commentaries; commentaries influenced heavily by Derridean deconstruction and by the legacy of Nietzsche's overcoming, and Heidegger's *Destruktion*, of metaphysics. Yet it is in a text of the later 1980s, *L'Expérience de la liberté* (1987), that Nancy demonstrates how the loss of philosophical foundation and a specific understanding of being social are, in fact, intimately interconnected or mutually imply each other. As such, *L'Expérience de la liberté*, connects the earlier deconstructive commentaries of the 1970s and early 1980s with Nancy's later mature ontology of the singular plural developed in the 1990s. It arguably acts as a key pivot between the two periods and, as such, is perhaps one of Nancy's most important and significant texts.

Arguably, Nancy takes Kant's critical philosophy as paradigmatic of philosophy per se insofar as he views the Kantian system as a very explicit becoming juridical of thought, that is to say, as an instance where philosophy explicitly positions itself as the arbiter, in a juridical manner, of the ground and limits of *all* human experience, of knowledge, reason, and judgment. At the very same time Kantian critical philosophy must therefore necessarily legitimate or ground itself *as philosophy* and must do so also in a juridical manner.[13] Yet this moment of autonomous self-legitimation or self-foundation is constituted in an instance of aporia, Nancy argues, one which un-grounds the entirety of the Kantian system in the very same moment that it seeks to give that system a firm foundation or ground.

The argument is first made at length in *Logodaedalus* in 1976. Here Nancy poses the question of presentation (or *Darstellung* in German) in relation to Kant's thought and, specifically, he poses the question of the style of philosophical presentation in the first *Critique*. He argues that Kant's attempt to render the style of philosophy akin to formal-mathematical proof, and to differentiate philosophical presentation from the vagaries of literary style, encounters a fundamental paradox. Seeking to found itself as a universal and necessary reasoning akin to mathematical proof and not as uncertain literary rhetoric or style, Kantian critique must assume or presuppose its ability to legislate for the difference between the two. Yet it must do so when, in fact, only the already successful act of legislating between mathematical and rhetorical *Darstellung* will confer upon it the very power to legislate. The argument he gives is complex and relies on, amongst other things, a close reading of the schematism in Kant and the pure power of the imagination as faculties of presentation or *Darstellung*.[14] But the paradox or aporia is straightforward: in order to legislate for itself as a strictly philosophical presentation, one which is decisively different from that of literature, and therefore to establish a foundation for itself *as* philosophy, philosophy must *already be* the very philosophy it seeks to legislate for, or ground itself as, and that it cannot yet be.

This argument is made once again in a slightly later essay 'Lapsus judicii' which dates from 1977 and is published in the 1983 volume 'L'Impératif catégorique.' Here though, Nancy articulates it in more obviously legal or juridical terms.[15] He does so by once more questioning the way in which the Kantian faculty of reason, as a power of legislation, legislates for its own power to

---

[13] Nancy, *L'Impératif catégorique* (Paris: Flammarion, 1983), 35.
[14] See Ian James, *The Fragmentary Demand: An Introduction to the Philosophy of Jean-Luc Nancy* (Stanford : Stanford University Press, 2006), 26–48.
[15] For an excellent discussion of the implications of this for legal thought, see Gilbert Leung 'Illegal Fictions' in *Jean-Luc Nancy: Justice, Legality, World*, ed. Benjamin Hutchens (London: Continuum, 2012), 82–95.

legislate. When reason reflects on itself, he argues, and on its own power and possibility, it does not encounter an object of experience or substantive property. Rather it encounters its own activity, an activity which it must take as a specific case to be legislated for. Nancy puts this in the following terms:

> Instead of possessing an essence—which would be that of knowing itself—reason knows only an accident—which is the instance of having to judge itself. Reason encounters its own case—the case of the judge.[16]

So the judge has to judge his own case in order to legitimate himself as judge. Yet in order to do so he already needs to be a judge and that he cannot yet be.

This, Nancy argues is a constitutive moment of philosophy as it seeks to ground itself in an explicitly legislative or juridical process of reason. Yet, as irreducibly aporetic, this moment of philosophy's self-constitution withdraws foundation, substance, and ground in the very gesture of its own self-grounding. Nancy puts this in the following terms:

> Because philosophy thinks itself—speaks itself—according to the law [*le droit*], it ineluctably thinks itself as structured (or as affected) by the *lapsus judicii*, by the slippage and the foundering [*la chute*] that are intrinsically at play in the absence of substance in which jurisdiction takes place.[17]

So where philosophy seeks the ground of its own self-certainty it finds, in the very execution and experience of philosophical reason itself, only an equivocation or uncertainty of ground: an appearance and withdrawal of its own foundation whose logic is in fact abyssal and predicated on a radical absence, a void of substance, and an experience of void.

This reading of Kant is taken forward by Nancy and developed further in *L'Expérience de la liberté*. Here the experience of absence, abyss, or void which reason undergoes in the gesture of its own self-foundation is linked to that other central Kantian concern, freedom. Nancy's understanding of Kantian critical philosophy (and here also of Hegel's speculative idealism) is once again mediated via an engagement with Heidegger and, in particular, Heidegger's

---

[16] Nancy, *L'Impératif catégorique*, 49.   [17] Nancy, *L'Impératif catégorique*, 55.

thinking of ground and truth.[18] In this context, the readings of Kant from the 1970s, and of philosophy's constitution in an instance of aporetic grounding/un-grounding, is taken as paradigmatic of a wider closure of metaphysics and of philosophy as it reaches the outer limit of its power and possibility. Nancy explicitly links philosophy's encounter with its own absence of ground with the impossibility of any philosophical determination of freedom as a ground for the will or for thought. Describing this in Heideggerian terms as an encounter with the internal limit of onto-theological discourse, Nancy remarks:

> This limit is reached as soon as the logic and signification of *foundation* in general, that is to say, of philosophy, is achieved. The end of philosophy deprives us of a foundation of freedom as much as it deprives us of freedom as a foundation.[19]

Kant's close alignment of reason with freedom within the architectonic of critical philosophy means that the aporia of ground or foundation that reason encounters also necessarily affects the experience of freedom. It may be worth highlighting in this context the manner in which Kantian reason operates in such a way as to affirm that we as humans are free from the conditioning influence of sensible experience and the limits that this may set on our possibilities of understanding. Reason is free in the sense that it is not limited by the world of nature and indeed, is in a certain sense, limitless. So when reason encounters its own absence of ground or foundation it, at the very same time, encounters also its autonomy, its unconditioned activity *as* reason, and does so *as* that very absence of ground. In this sense the failure of reason to found itself is not simply its abolition or simply its negation in favour of the triumph of other heteronomous forces or principles. Its encounter with its own absence of foundation is also a discovery of the very condition of its own autonomy and freedom, that is to say, the absence of its determination or conditioning by a substantive

---

[18] See Martin Heidegger, *Kant and the Problem of Metaphysics*, trans. Richard Taft (Bloomington: Indiana University Press, 1990); see also 'On the Essence of Ground' and 'On the essence of Truth' in Martin Heidegger, *Pathmarks*, ed. William McNeill (Cambridge: Cambridge University Press: 1998), 97–135, 136–54.

[19] Nancy, *The Experience of Freedom*, trans. Bridget McDonald (Stanford: Stanford University Press, 1993), 12; *L'Expérience de la liberté* (Paris : Galilée, 1987), 16. All references will be given first to the English translation and then to the original French edition.

ground or by any other instance. Reason's absence of ground and reason's freedom, that is to say, the free activity of reason as reason, are constituted in the very same aporetic moment, a moment of simultaneously (freed) possibility and (un-grounded) impossibility.

Given that what is at stake here is not simply and solely the faculty of reason, nor simply and solely the autonomy of the will but, within the systematic scope of Kant's architectonic, the entirety of human experience and knowledge and its universal and necessary conditions of possibility, this moment of aporia has an ontological, rather than, say, simply epistemological, force. Freedom in this context is not just the *operation* of reason unfettered by the limits of sensible experience, rather, for Nancy, it is the experience of existence itself *as* unconditioned by any ground or foundation, by any substance or essence. This ontological understanding of freedom underpins the argument of *L'Expérience de la liberté* as a whole and is articulated very explicitly: 'Freedom,' Nancy writes, 'perhaps designates nothing more and nothing less than existence itself.'[20]

So when philosophical reason or onto-theology is brought to the internal limit of its possibility, this limit being the ineluctable encounter with the aporia of its own self-constitution or self-grounding, then it also necessarily encounters the void of an existence which is without ground or substance. In the absence of any ground it experiences the existence of freedom or, more properly, it experiences existence *as* freedom. At this internal limit philosophy's power to legislate for its own power to legislate is interrupted or thrown into hiatus. With this, and necessarily, its power to determine an image of the human and therefore to account for human sociability on the basis of any ground or foundation is suspended also. And yet, and this is arguably the centre-point of all Nancy's thinking and his originality as a thinker, it is in this precise moment of the experience of abyssal freedom, groundlessness, and void that an understanding of relationality and of being social in fact emerges. Nancy articulates this in the following terms:

> At the limit of philosophy, there where we are, having not made our way exactly, but having happened there, and finding ourselves still happening there, there is only ... the free dissemination of existence.

[20] Nancy, *Experience of Freedom*, 14, 18.

> This free dissemination is ... the anarchy ... of a singular and thus in essence plural arising whose being *as being* is neither ground, nor element, nor reason, but truth, which would amount to saying, in this instance, freedom.[21]

Nancy insists throughout *L'Expérience de la liberté* that the encounter with the limit of philosophy or onto-theology results necessarily from the initial of decision of philosophy itself and its constitutive aporia.[22] At the very same time he argues that existence emerges, arises or is encountered in the experience of this limit as necessarily free, and in this as necessarily both singular and plural. Formal ontology, he argues, has one of two choices: either being is singular in and of itself, that is, it has one underlying principle or ground in which all multiplicity is absorbed, or, on the other hand, all the multiplicity that exists, exists only in its irreducibly multiple singularity: 'there is no being apart from singularity: each time just this once, and there would be nothing general or common except the "each time just this once."'[23]

Nancy's reasoning aims to trace and follow the path and the fatality of philosophical reason itself, moving from the experience of a constitutive absence of ground, void, or abyss, to an experience of freedom, and from there to the necessity of a formal ontology of singular plurality. In this context the thinking of a fundamental ontological relationality, what he elsewhere calls 'being-with,' emerges as a direct correlate of the experience of existence as free, as singular and plural. Nancy expresses this as follows: 'The linking or interlinking of relations doubtless does not proceed from freedom, but is contemporaneous and coextensive with it ... singular being is in relation or according to relation,' or in more direct terms, 'singularity is immediately in relation.'[24] This is a mode of relationality which does not root itself in any substance, ground, or shared essence on the basis of which singularities could come into relation with each other. Rather it is a relationality which emerges in and as the freedom of existence, the ungrounded 'each time just this once' of an existence, which can only singularize itself or exist *as* a 'just this once' in relation to other singular instances given

---

[21] Nancy, *Experience of Freedom*, 12–13, 16–17 [translation modified].
[22] Nancy, *Experience of Freedom*, 7, 47.
[23] Nancy, *Experience of Freedom*, 67, 91–2.
[24] Nancy, *Experience of Freedom*, 66, 91 and 67, 92.

each time just this once. In this way Nancy comes to think of the existence of that which exists always in terms of singularity and plurality but also in terms of the sharing of singularity, its existence in relation or in-common.

The Human, the Non-human

Nancy's thinking of being-with, his ontology of the singular plural, and their elaboration in texts such as *La Communauté désœuvrée* (1986) and *Être singulier pluriel* (1996) are perhaps the best known aspects of his thought. Yet, within the broader reception of Nancean thought, the relative neglect of *L'Expérience de la liberté*, arguably one of his most difficult and also most rigorous texts, means that the specific path of thinking that leads him from the deconstructive commentaries of Kant in the 1970s to the thinking of ontology, sense, and world in the 1990s has not been discerned as clearly as it might have been. Understanding *L'Expérience de la liberté* in relation to the earlier 1970s commentaries on Kant and as a rigorous and necessary development from them, allows the interdependence of key elements of Nancean thinking to be clearly discerned: the experience of ontological groundlessness, of freedom or void, and the disclosure of a fundamental relationality of singular plural existence, emerge in and as the fate of philosophy as it encounters the internal limit of its power and possibility and does so insofar as 'it was lead to that point by the initial decision of philosophy itself.'[25]

This discussion began, taking Hume and Kant as exemplary figures, by arguing that philosophy can account for human sociability only on the basis of the specific images of the human that it offers and on the basis of its capacity, as philosophy, to legislate for, to determine, and to ground the human in general and as such. Nancy's thinking shows that an understanding of ontological relationality, of being social, is not only possible but follows necessarily from the suspension of philosophy's legislative power, and from the exposure to a fundamental absence of ontological ground. Yet the question arises as to how this thinking of ontological relationality, of being-in-common or of being-with, can be more concretely developed as a thinking of human relations and

---

[25] Nancy, *Experience of Freedom*, 47.

of human sociality or sociability. For, exposed to the suspension of its power to lay a foundation and brought to its moment of closure or end, philosophy cannot give an image of the human or of human nature. The groundless, 'each time just this once' of singular plural existence would disqualify absolutely any general idea of a universally shared human essence, substance or nature, or any universally applicable image of the human as such. And yet Nancy refers to or invokes the name of the human often in his writing, not least in *L'Expérience de la liberté*. He also, as has been remarked upon very critically by Derrida, uses terms such as 'fraternity' to describe social being and solidarity, terms which carry the historic weight of a very specific, and specifically (male) gendered figuration of the human.[26] Yet Nancy's use of the term 'human' needs to be qualified by, and understood in the light of, the following important passage from *L'Expérience de la liberté*:

> 'According to the archi-register of sharing, which is also that of singularity's 'each time,' there is no 'human being.' ... In the relation [of singularity], 'human being' is not given—but it is only the relation which can give its 'humanity.' Now it is freedom which gives relation in the withdrawal of being. It is therefore freedom that gives humanity and not the inverse. But the gift that freedom gives is never, insofar as it is the gift of freedom, a quality, property or essence of the order of humanitas.[27]

There is no 'human being' and the 'human' can never be thought as a quality, property, or essence. The implications of these sentences are worth dwelling upon. For they suggest that, if one is to think the term 'human' in the context of Nancy's thought in general then, strictly speaking, it can never take as its predicate *any* given image of human nature or essence, nor *any* given image of the human per se, even a residual, hollowed out, or vestigial understanding of what may be irreducible to finite 'human' existence or what we normally designate as humanity or homo sapiens.[28] The human in

---

[26] On this, see Derrida, *Voyous* (Paris: Galilée, 2003), 88–93.

[27] Nancy, *Experience of Freedom*, 73, 99.

[28] Martin Crowley in *L'Homme Sans* (Paris: Lignes, 2009) has argued powerfully for a vestigial, foundationless conception of the irreducibly human that can be derived from Nancy's work. Nancy's response to Crowley in the post-face to this work respectfully takes some distance from this argument: '"The human without" is so barely predicable that I would happily add this: it is not even predicable by "the human,"' 182. Crowley's very fine reading of Nancy and his argument for a politics of finitude situates this ves-

Nancy would necessarily have as its predicate a radical absence of *any* image or essence of humanity, it would indicate only a plurality of singular ungrounded existences and their relationality alone.

This implies that, in Nancy's tracing of the fate of Kantian reason, a radically non-human thinking can be discerned. From its aporetic self-constitution, to its experience of groundlessness and freedom, through to its experience of existence as relational singular plurality, reason here is not functioning within the orbit of the human since it cannot in any way know what the human in its essence or nature might be in the first instance. In a more recent text Nancy says of Kantian reason that it: 'is not anthropomorphic, in particular not psychological or social, and in the end not human. Or the human in it is not given but prescribed.'[29] This is consistent with his earlier remark in *L'Expérience de la liberté* cited above that 'it is freedom that gives humanity and not the inverse.' In terms of the thinking of relation, being-with, or being social the implication is clear. Nancy gives us no grounds whatsoever, and indeed no philosophical means, to limit the thinking of being-with or being social to what we might traditionally conceive of as human. If 'singularity is in relation' and it is 'only the relation which can give [it] its "humanity,"' then what we may come to *prescribe* as human when we come to think of ontological and then social relationality in Nancean terms will include every and any singularity, whether it be traditionally conceived of as human or non-human, as organic or inorganic, as animate or as inanimate.

The Ground of Being Social

Recent critical-philosophical responses to Nancy's thought have sought to develop the implications of his ungrounded relational ontology by questioning the extent to which it can be taken as a starting point for any thinking of politics, of ethics, or of justice and juridical thought respectively. So, for instance, Martin Crowley in *L'Homme sans* [*The Human Without*] offers a powerful and important account of the way in which Nancy's thinking, and the general trajectory of twentieth-century French thought within

tigial conception of the human within a broader trajectory of post-war French thought including figures such as Bataille, Blanchot, Camus, Antelme and Dionys Mascolo.

[29] Jean-Luc Nancy, 'From the Imperative to Law' in *Jean-Luc Nancy: Justice, Legality, World*, ed. B. C. Hutchens (London: Continuum, 2012), 11–18, 14.

which it can be situated, might yield something like an egalitarian politics of finitude and how they may offer ontologically motivated imperatives towards an active politics of equality.[30] Daniele Rugo's *Jean-Luc Nancy and the Thinking of Otherness* has sought to demonstrate, through detailed readings of Nancy alongside Heidegger and Levinas, that his thinking can yield something like a fundamental ethics rooted in the specificity of relations to and with singularity.[31] Or again, Benjamin Hutchens' edited volume, *Jean-Luc Nancy: Justice, Legality World* presents a number of essays which attempt to show that a thinking of justice and a singular plural ontology necessarily and mutually imply each other.[32] What this discussion has demonstrated is that any politics, ethics, or notion of justice that takes Nancy's singular plural ontology as their starting point cannot, of course, take this ontology as a ground or foundation for politics, ethics, or justice. Moreover, and this point has been less developed in responses to Nancy's thought, any such politics, ethics, or notion of justice must operate in the radical absence of any given or determinate image of the human and in no way restrict or limit itself to the sphere or orbit of the human, however it may be conceived.[33] As has been suggested, the absence of ground encountered in Nancy's encounter with the limits and end of philosophy gives no ground whatsoever for doing so. If ontological relationality can yield political or ethical demands and motivate demands for justice then these will be demands made to and in the name of singularity and the responsibilities that may impose themselves in and through the primordial relations between singularities, 'human' or non-human, organic or inorganic, animate or inanimate.

This argument opens the way for understanding Nancy's formulations around community, being-with, sense, and world in terms of a broader non-human philosophy of nature in which sociability, ethical responsibility, and political solidarity or community must

[30] Crowley, *L'Homme sans*, see n. 29.

[31] Daniele Rugo, *Jean-Luc Nancy and the Thinking of Otherness* (London: Bloomsbury, 2013).

[32] Hutchens, *Jean-Luc Nancy*, see n. 15 above; see also and in particular the essays by James 'The Just Measure,' and Watkin 'Ontology and Incommensurability in Nancy's Notion of Justice,' 19–46.

[33] Crowley gives an excellent discussion of how a politics of finitude based on a groundless vestigial figure of the human might affirm solidarity with animals; see *L'Homme sans*, 127–56.

be thought in non-species specific terms. Such terms would neither be residually human, post-human, trans-human, or anti-human, but radically non-human in the sense that, at the starting point, no image of the human whatsoever offers itself as given. Here the experience of world, and the sharing of the sense of the world, would not just be the world of human finitude, sense and meaning, or means and ends such as we may have conceived them to date. Rather it would be an ontologically ungrounded social being, or being social, whose limits or criteria of belonging cannot be philosophically grounded or prescribed in any way. The prescription, the belonging, would come from the freedom of existence, the arising or appearing of singularities alone and the relations that are concretely made out of this co-appearing. If we follow Nancy to think the ground of being social in a necessary opening of an absence of ground, then we must do so in the name of an existence or thought which 'is not anthropomorphic ... and in the end not human.'

— 2 —

Being Social in 'Law and Society'

Peter Fitzpatrick

When much is asked, more is left out.

— J. Erpenbeck[1]

The still-burgeoning scholarship of 'law and society' presents us with a productive impasse. In one corner of the field, we find law as the creature of society or of forces operating through society. In another corner, law takes on an insistent autonomy in which it shapes, orders, even creates society—to borrow standard attributions. Yet an analysis of 'society' in a modern sense shows law occupying both sides of that divide. Such a seemingly contrary condition of law takes it beyond its relation to this modern society and renders it intrinsic, even equivalent, to sociality, a law both delimited by and insistently impelled beyond a determinate society.

Society

First, a conspectus of the 'society' invoked here: a conspectus derived from Foucault's integrating the formation of liberal and neoliberal economies with the emergence of 'governmentality'—a

---

[1] Jenny Erpenbeck, *Visitation*, trans. Susan Bernofsky (London: Portobello Books, 2010), 92.

pervasive and tentacular governing of whole populations. In turn, this 'liberal governmentality' entails an

> omnipresent government, a government which nothing escapes, a government which conforms to the rules of right, and a government which nevertheless respects the specificity of the economy, ... [and] a government that manages civil society, the nation, society, the social.[2]

Yet in being managed, society is not comprehensibly subordinated: 'there is indeed always something in the social body ... which in some sense escapes relations of power.'[3] It is the same 'civil society' that enables the 'governability' of individuals within 'the liberal art of government.'[4]

Indeed an ever unlimited sway of government would be the antithesis of liberalism as normally understood, and Foucault does stress that 'the form of governmental technology we call liberalism ... [has] its own self-limitation' as its objective.[5] That self-limitation in turn 'is pegged to the specificity of economic procedures' and to 'economic naturalness.'[6] With the 'economic world' being 'naturally opaque and naturally non-totalizable,' there is no social bound that could delimit it.[7] As with an unlimited governmentality, however, the part of society is not inconsequential, for here civil society provides the 'field of reference' in which the liberal art of government combines 'governing economically' and 'governing juridically.'[8] And it is within and as such a society that individuals are 'governable insofar as a new ensemble can be defined which will envelop them both as subjects of right and as economic actors.'[9] Governing juridically relates to more than the subjects of right. Foucault conceived also of the sovereign state as 'juridical'—a state able to 'see to the management of civil society.'[10]

---

[2] Michel Foucault, *The Birth of Biopolitics: Lectures at the Collège de France 1978–1979*, trans. Graham Burchell (Basingstoke: Palgrave Macmillan, 2008), 296.

[3] Michel Foucault, 'Power and Strategies.' Interview conducted by editorial collective of *Les révoltes logiques* in Michel Foucault, *Power/Knowledge: Selected Interviews and Other Writings 1972: 1977*, trans. Colin Gordon and others (Brighton: The Harvester Press, 1980), 138.

[4] Foucault, *Birth of Biopolitics*, 295.   [5] Foucault, *Birth of Biopolitics*, 296, 197.

[6] Foucault, *Birth of Biopolitics*, 21–2, 297.   [7] Foucault, *Birth of Biopolitics*, 282.

[8] Foucault, *Birth of Biopolitics*, 295.   [9] Foucault, *Birth of Biopolitics*, 295.

[10] Foucault, *Birth of Biopolitics*, 283; Michel Foucault, *Security, Territory, Population: Lectures at the Collège de France 1977–1978*, trans. Graham Burchell (Basingstoke:

This governing conglomerate will provide our *mise en scène*, but for now I want to focus on the seemingly contrary part, or parts, which 'society' plays in it. This society enables a generalized 'governability' and provides a formative 'field of reference' for a governing economically, yet that same society is a vacuity abjectly taking its content from them. It could hardly be otherwise. If it is responsively to absorb their illimitability, such a society can have no contrary content of its own even as it would itself have to be illimitable.

That division, which is somehow also not a division, is played out in depictions of modern society. Raymond Williams' compact genealogy would see 'society' divided between an 'active and immediate' sense and a 'general and abstract sense' and, in a way that could be mapped onto Foucault's accounts of the emergence of governmentality, he finds from the sixteenth century a 'strengthening' of the general and abstract leading to its becoming predominant from the late eighteenth century.[11] With the advent of the 'crucial notion of civil society ... society was confirmed in its most general and eventually abstract senses.'[12]

In a like vein, Lefort traces the emergence of a modern society the existence of which no longer relies on a transcendent realm beyond, a society which in its self-sufficiency is 'transparent to itself' or 'intelligible in itself'; there is 'an illusion which lies at the heart of modern society: namely that the institution of the social can account for itself.'[13] Then there are more straightforward declamations that fall on one side of the divide or the other. Society can be the comprehensively subordinate creation of economy, for example. Or it can be comprehensively determining of, say, its members' identities in varieties of 'social constructionism.'[14]

Which leaves 'society' seemingly mired in existential incoherence. If society is to take on any enduringly positive determinacy, it cannot be constantly illimitable. And vice versa. A resolution of a kind is encapsulated by Nietzsche's supremely sane madman

Palgrave Macmillan, 2007), 350.

[11] Raymond Williams, 'Society' in *Keywords: A vocabulary of culture and society* (London: Fontana Press, 1976), 291–2.

[12] Williams, 'Society,' 293.

[13] Claude Lefort, *The Political Forms of Modern Society: Bureaucracy, Democracy, Totalitarianism* (Cambridge: Polity Press, 1986) 184, 201, 207, and generally chapter 6.

[14] Irving Velody, 'Unnatural Acts—Or Nature Expelled from Her Garden: How Constructionism Came to Pass,' *History of the Human Sciences* 7 (1994) 81–5.

in announcing the death of God, a deicide that we have brought about yet a deed that 'is still more remote to [us] than the remotest stars.'[15] We are thence left 'straying as though through an infinite nothing,' left in the darkening 'shadows of god,' left with the imperative of having to invent for ourselves 'festivals of atonement'—at-one-ment, the recovering of a unity—and 'sacred games.'[16] For Nietzsche, a significant sacred game would seem to be 'the new idol' of the state, the state that assumes the competence of 'the ordaining finger of God.'[17] That assumption, as with society, has the state fusing the incipiently illimitable with the determinately existent. And the match is also more intimate with 'the modern nation state' providing the typical configuration of 'the general theory of social integration'—'a methodological nationalism.'[18] That makes state and society two players of the sacred game, two deific substitutes asserting a transcendent competence by absorbing the illimitable into its determinate or determining being—a competence of a markedly monotheistic kind. The impossibility of a shared monotheism is surpassed by this matching of a paradigm society with the nation state, a sovereign state. That co-existent pantheon is made operative through a further resolution, of a kind.

Such a resolution involves society's being aligned with that negative universal reference which goes to constitute an occidental modernity. This reference, in absorbing Nietzsche's 'infinite nothing,' evades ultimate resort to a most unmodern transcendent positivity.[19] As Heidegger's commentary on Nietzsche's parable has it,

> even if God ... has vanished from his place in the supersensory world, still the place itself is preserved, although it has become empty. ...

---

[15] Friedrich Nietzsche, *The Gay Science*, trans. Josefine Nauckhoff (Cambridge: Cambridge University Press, 2001), 120 (§ 125).

[16] Nietzsche, *Gay Science*, 120 (§ 125), 110 (§109). In Nauckhoff's translation *heilig* is rendered as 'holy' but here 'sacred' is preferred as more befitting a deific substitute.

[17] Friedrich Nietzsche, 'On the New Idol,' in *Thus Spoke Zarathustra*, trans. Adrian del Caro (Cambridge: Cambridge University Press, 2006), 34–5. And for the 'finger of God,' see also *Exodus* 31:18.

[18] Respectively, Johann P. Arnason, 'Nationalism, Globalization and Modernity,' in *Global Culture: Nationalism, Globalization and Modernity*, ed. Mike Featherstone (London: Sage, 1990), 224, and Andreas Wimmer and Nina Glick Schiller, 'Methodological nationalism and beyond: nation-state building, migration and the social sciences,' *Global Networks* 2 (2002), 302.

[19] Nietzsche, *Gay Science*, 120 (§ 125).

The empty place even invites its own re-occupation and calls for the God who disappeared from it to be replaced by another.[20]

Such 'another,' whether nation state or society, becomes what certain alterities, certain 'others,' are not. Or it becomes not what certain alterities are. Being entirely negative and universal in range, the division and exclusion are complete. What is beyond the universal can only be utterly beyond. Hence, and for example, there is racism and the irreducible alterity of the relegated race. Yet that very appropriation of a universality has, as universal, to be all-inclusive as well. So the negative universal reference generates an antithesis that then includes that antithesis within itself. The now-included take on an operative part within the universal scheme whilst still being excluded from it. Thereafter Heidegger's deific replacement imports a negative theology—not the quest for a presence some revelation of which is assiduously sought, but the elevation of an absence voiding enquiry.

Here we could return briefly to Foucault and governmentality. Such governmentality entailed the pervasive conjunction of biopower and disciplinary power—a conjunction encompassing the 'life' of a society and the lives of its members.[21] In a trajectory that for Foucault emanated from racism—racial division providing 'the first, historico-political discourse on society'—biopower and discipline created the 'abnormal,' the 'anomaly,' the deviant, and these provide the formative force of the socially normal and the socially conforming.[22] The abnormal and such are both 'interior and foreign,' subjected to 'an inclusion through exclusion.'[23]

All of which may seem to take matters no further than one side of society's part in the conglomerate of power mapped by Foucault—society as the functional extension of something else, of such a normalising disciplinary power: 'society *means* that norms

---

[20] Martin Heidegger, 'Nietzsche's Word: "God is Dead",' in *Off the Beaten Track*, trans. Julian Young and Kenneth Haynes (Cambridge: Cambridge University Press, 2002), 168.

[21] Michel Foucault, *'Society Must Be Defended,'* trans. David Macey (London: Allen Lane, 2003), 242–3; Foucault, *Security, Territory*, 55, 104, 108–9; Foucault, *Birth of Biopolitics*, 15–16.

[22] e.g. Michel Foucault, *Discipline and Punish: The Birth of the Prison*, trans. Alan Sheridan (Harmondsworth: Penguin, 1979), 229; Foucault, 'Society Must...,' 49.

[23] Michel Foucault, 'Truth and Juridical Forms,' in *Essential Works of Foucault 1954–1984 Vol.3: Power* (London: Penguin, 2001), 78.

regulate human conduct.'[24] Yet there was another 'society' in that conglomerate, one on which other powers depended for their realization. And aptly enough, this society has its own generative basis in the negative universal reference. With this version, a 'modern' occidental society is constituently set against a fictive society which it encapsulates yet rejects, whether that be a religionized and 'dark' medieval society or varieties of barbaric or savage society excluded from a universalized civility.[25] This is the supposed outcome of a progressive development of society, more specifically 'the concrete development of *bürgerliche Gesellschaft*: market society, civil society, bourgeois society. Only then did the generality society become visible.'[26] This 'generality' corresponds to the 'general and abstract sense' which Williams finds definitive of modern 'society' in its pervasive dominance over 'active and immediate senses.'[27] And it is the negative universal reference that frees this 'general and abstract' society from any persistent positivity and endows it with a capacity of illimitable appropriation.

Law and Society I

Among the ranks of the appropriated, law has a specific prominence. In the field of law and society, law is often conceived of as the entirely dependent offspring of society, and so much so that the social configuration changes to one supposedly inhospitable to law, such as a society pervaded by regulation and 'bureaucratic law.'[28] Scarcely less draconic are those theories that would cast law in functional or instrumental abjection to the encompassing cause of society. Yet, by way of partial relief, there is a persistent strand of law and society which, whilst recognising some such constituent force of society, would endow law with some distinctness and efficacy, with an autonomy even if 'relative,' or with some viability even in highly repressive societies.[29]

[24] Ralf Dahrendorf, 'On the Origin of Inequality among Men,' in *Social Inequality*, ed. André Béteille (Harmondsworth: Penguin, 1969), 38, his emphasis.

[25] Constantin Fasolt, *The Limits of History* (Chicago: The University of Chicago Press, 2004), 18–19, 219.

[26] David Frisby and Derek Sayer, *Society* (Chichester: Ellis Horwood, 1986), 121.

[27] Williams, *Keywords*, 291, 293.

[28] e.g. Roberto Mangabeira Unger, *Law in Modern Society: Toward a Criticism of Social Theory* (New York: The Free Press, 1976), 238.

[29] e.g. Isaac D. Balbus, 'Commodity Form and Legal Form: An Essay on the 'Relative

These indulgences could be seen as an attenuation of something which, for our purposes, is more telling—the seeming imperative for society itself to generate an autonomy for law. And with the type of modern society inhabiting this chapter so far, law does arrive at a position of differentiated autonomy. In liberal or neoliberal society, law provides the link between society's now disparate members: 'In the midst of strangers, law reaches its highest level'; 'the progress of law consists in the destruction of every natural tie, in a continued process of separation and isolation.'[30] Or, aptly enough, in the Marxist perspective provided by Pashukanis: 'the fundamental condition of existence of the legal form is rooted in the very economic organization of society'; but in a way that affirms 'the deep interconnection between the legal form and the commodity form.' This economic organization establishes the law as well as subjecting it.[31]

Coming to a final furrow in the field of law and society, law's established distinctness is heightened even as it remains formatively tied to society. The connection is deftly explored by Nonet and Selznick in their *Toward Responsive Law: Law & Society in Transition*.[32] This transition is staged by way of '[a] social science approach,' sketching the progressive 'development' of

> three modalities of basic 'states' of law-in-society: (1) law as a servant of repressive power, (2) law as a differentiated [and restricted] institution capable of taming repression and protecting its own integrity [autonomous law], and (3) law as a facilitator of response to social needs and aspirations.[33]

What is most distinctive in this typology, and the authors' ultimate concern, is 'a responsive legal order, more open to social

---

Autonomy' of Law,' *Law & Society Review* 11 (1977): 571; Otto Kirchheimer, *Political Justice: The Use of Legal Procedure for Political Ends* (Princeton: Princeton University Press, 1961), 421–3.

[30] Respectively, Donald Black, *The Behaviour of Law* (New York: Academic Press, 1976), 41 and Jhering as quoted in Stanley Diamond, *In Search of the Primitive: A Critique of Civilization* (New Brunswick: Transaction Books, 1974), 261.

[31] Evgeny Pashukanis, *Law and Marxism: A General Theory* (London: Ink Links, 1978), 63.

[32] Philippe Nonet and Philip Selznick, *Responsive Law: Law & Society in Transition* (New Brunswick: Transaction Publishers, 2001).

[33] Nonet and Selznick, *Responsive Law*, 9, 14–15, 18–19.

influence and more effective in dealing with social problems.'[34] There is, however, the risk that such an instrumentally responsive law can lose the limiting and 'insular safety of autonomous law,' becoming 'too open' and losing 'the ability to moderate the role of power in society,' and becoming as well an acute instance of 'the dilemma of integrity and openness.'[35] Yet responsiveness, obviously, cannot be simply craven. If it were, and given what Foucault would call law's 'infinitely accommodating welcome,' law would dissipate in the response.[36] Further, with any law some responsive capacity is needful if law is at all to accommodate the ever-changing conditions to which it must relate. The alternative is a staid irrelevance. What becomes imperative here, returning to Nonet and Selznick, is a responsive 'capacity for responsible, and hence discriminate and selective adaptation. A responsive institution retains a grasp on what is essential to its integrity while taking account of new forces in its environment.'[37]

The 'dilemma of integrity and openness,' as Nonet and Selznick aptly note, 'is not unique to law: All institutions experience a conflict between integrity and openness.'[38] A similar 'dilemma' occupied that instituted modern society sketched earlier. This 'abstract' society found itself taking on an illimitable openness to such powers, yet that very illimitability ensured its not being ultimately bounded by those powers. From that position of 'openness,' as it were, society stood apart from that which it would effect, yet in so doing there is a compliant connection with its situated determinacy, with its 'integrity.'[39] The assertion of this integrity entailed a drawing of the illimitable into the determinate—a transcendent affirmation at odds with society in and as a secular modernity. That disparity is avoided in society's taking on identity by way of a negative universal reference and in this 'abstract' way eschewing resort to a positively transcendent affirmation. Inexorably, this

---

[34] Nonet and Zelznick, *Responsive Law*, 72.

[35] Nonet and Zelznick, *Responsive Law*, 74, 76.

[36] Michel Foucault, "Maurice Blanchot: The Thought from Outside." Translated by Brian Massumi, in Michel Foucault and Maurice Blanchot, *Foucault/Blanchot*, (New York: Zone Books, 1987), 38.

[37] Nonet and Selznick, *Responsive Law*, 77.

[38] Nonet and Zelznick, *Towards Responsive Law*, 76. Of course, and as well, this common quality is itself generative of difference. Law's difference will be further explored later in this chapter.

[39] For the terms, see Nonet and Zelznick, *Responsive Law*, 76.

resolution would fail when society's effects needed to be rendered and affirmed positively and enforcedly, whence a transcendent determination would be called for.[40]

What impels the relation between law and modern society is this block on society's forming an enforceable positive determination. And what the scholarship of law and society reveals is a modern law oriented towards integrity, towards a 'unity,' towards an autonomous distinctness from society, yet a law oriented also towards a responsive openness to society—to whatever society is or may come to be. As with society in the service of other powers, this responsiveness calls for law to be illimitably open, and in its illimitability it stands apart from that which it otherwise serves. And it is in such standing apart that law provides the transcendent point from which positive determination can flow. Law's illimitability, its generative inability to be fixed to any positivity, enables it to effect a transcendence that is 'pure' in its not being implicated with any transcendence that is enduringly positive—a law that, as Blanchot has it, 'affirms itself as law and without reference to anything higher: to it alone, pure transcendence.'[41] This transcendent, illimitable law cannot be ultimately rendered as the posited, the positive, bonded offspring of anything else.

Law and Society II

To leave matters there, aligning law with a type of modern society, may merely refine that tenet of law and society which would see law comprehensively constructed by society. Yet the law inhabiting this constraining society was itself necessarily illimitable and as such stood apart from that society. This embeds the possibility and prospect of law escaping 'the already established, already stifling reign of society,' and doing so in a way congruent with 'society' in its illimitability.[42] Yet further, and as far as this chapter has ranged, law could still be no more than the emanation of a particular type

---

[40] The positive is also effected in scientistic affirmations through such as biopower and disciplinary power, yet a societal deficit remains, one which (anticipating now the next paragraph above) is filled by law; see Foucault, *Birth of Biopolitics*, 37 and Ben Golder and Peter Fitzpatrick, *Foucault's Law* (Abingdon: Routledge, 2009), chapter 2.

[41] Maurice Blanchot, *The Step Not Beyond*, trans. Lycette Nelson (New York: State University of New York Press, 1992), 25.

[42] Jean-Luc Nancy, *The Inoperative Community*, trans. Peter Connor et al. (Minneapolis: University of Minnesota Press, 1991), 17 for the quotation.

of modern society. But law not only emanates from but has to surpass this type of society. It would, then, need to have a force apart from, yet immanent, to that society. So, this anfractuous connection between law and society would intimate a relation beyond its particularity.

Some such relation inheres in Rousseau's finding law intrinsic to 'the social contract,' a law having to pre-exist the contract for the realized society to be at all.[43] Society as a determinate yet protean 'people' or 'nation' presupposes a law endowed by a 'lawgiver,' one whom the secular modern would not at first find amenable since, as Rousseau announces, 'Gods would be needed to give men laws.'[44] Yet, even though the lawgiver's 'task ... is beyond human powers,' it is a task the achievement of which Rousseau sees as necessary in the world.[45] It is also a task that Rousseau configures to the qualities of the lawgiver. In bestowing the laws of the constitution, the lawgiver has to create a social bond that integrates individuals into it, a bond believed in by those individuals and one that is 'lasting.'[46] To perform those tasks, the lawgiver has to be quite apart from the people being so endowed and lacking in any authority, right, force, or interest in creating the laws. From that unconditional position apart, the lawgiver has to exhibit 'a superior intelligence' and have a 'great soul,' and much more.[47] These attributes, however, are but analogies for a dimension of law drained of attachment to, and constantly attuned beyond, the existent. And in all: 'Laws are really nothing other than the conditions on which civil association exists.'[48]

There is an affinity between this law of Rousseau's and perceptions of law in poststructural philosophy. So, Derrida would find a 'law of originary sociability' in 'the relation to the other,' a relation 'prior to all organised *socius*, ... [p]rior to all *determined* law ... but not prior to law *in general*,' this law of originary sociability being 'also a law, perhaps the very essence of law.'[49] And this

---

[43] Jean-Jacques Rousseau, *The Social Contract*, trans. Maurice Cranston (London: Penguin Books, 1968), 87.

[44] Rousseau, Social Contract, 87.   [45] Rousseau, *Social Contract*, 86.

[46] Rousseau, *Social Contract*, 84–5, 87, 99.   [47] Rousseau, *Social Contract*, 84, 87.

[48] Rousseau, *Social Contract*, 83; translation of *l'association civile* changed from 'civil society.'

[49] Jacques Derrida, *Politics of Friendship*, trans. George Collins (London: Verso, 1997), 231, his emphasis.

sociability permeates law enduringly as an origin that 'must repeat itself originarily, must alter itself to count *as origin*, that is to say, to preserve itself.'[50]

A more situated sense of this law could be derived from Derrida's concern with a quality inherent to being social—that of hospitality. For Derrida hospitality is imperatively unconditional:

> Only an unconditional hospitality can give meaning and practical rationality to a concept of hospitality. Unconditional hospitality exceeds juridical, political, or economic calculation. But no thing and no one happens or arrives without it.[51]

Yet a conditional or conditioned hospitality is also imperative:

> The unconditional law of hospitality needs the [conditional/conditioned] laws, it *requires* them. This demand is constitutive. It wouldn't be effectively unconditional, the law, if it didn't *have to become* effective, concrete, determined.[52]

In sum, '[p]olitical, juridical, and ethical responsibilities have their place, if they take place, only in this transaction ... between these two hospitalities, the unconditional and the conditional.'[53] Without more, the unconditional, the illimitably responsive, law of hospitality would be a mere dissipation. That law would, then, depend on the conditioned laws to give it determinate effect. The determinate laws, in turn, depend on the unconditional law, the responsive law, for their own continuing existence. Bluntly, law has to be a realized determinacy yet illimitably responsive to what may yet be. These dimensions of law 'in their very heterogeneity ... are undissociable.'[54]

---

[50] Jacques Derrida, 'Force of Law: The "Mystical Foundation of Authority",' trans. Mary Quaintance, in Jacques Derrida, *Acts of Religion* (New York: Routledge, 2002) 277–8, his emphasis. My engagement with law continues to escape, none too surreptitiously, into a generality of law that would take it beyond a tie to any particular kind of society.

[51] Jacques Derrida, *Rogues: Two Essays on Reason*, trans. Pascale-Ann Brault and Michael Naas (Stanford: Stanford University Press, 2005), 149.

[52] Jacques Derrida, *Of Hospitality*, trans. Rachel Bowlby (Stanford: Stanford University Press, 2000), 79, his emphasis.

[53] Jacques Derrida, 'Autoimmunity: Real and Symbolic Suicide: A Dialogue with Jacques Derrida,' in Giovanna Borradori, *Philosophy in a Time of Terror: Dialogues with Jürgen Habermas and Jacques Derrida* (Chicago: The University of Chicago Press, 2003), 130.

[54] Derrida, 'Force of Law,' 257.

Returning to law and society then, we have a law that melds into both of its disparate strands. With one, there is a determinate law that is somehow apart from and impacts on society. With the other, we have a law that is intrinsically responsive to and derivative from society. There is a continuate coming together inextricably of these two elements in and as legal determination—determination not just as the particular decision or enactment, but also as the conceptual configuring of determinations that make up the ever mutable 'legal system' and the ever mutable types or areas of law. Determination then may seem 'positively' to set what law is. Such determinations can be conspicuously enduring. Occidental law, for example, has for long found its paradigm in the law of the nation-state. Somewhat less conspicuously, and returning to Foucault's sketch of liberal society, the law's reach can be decidedly inhibited when it comes to affecting either the economy or the domains of biopower and disciplinary power.[55] Yet law as sociality cannot be ultimately inhibited and any constricting determination is only ever 'for the time being.' In this, and as Derrida has it, law exhibits 'the non-contemporaneity with itself of the living present.'[56] And the ever-frustrated jurisprudential search for what law 'is' endures.

It may aid philosophical assertion to illustrate law's insubordinate relation to a modern society which takes its paradigm branding from the nation and its state—a 'sovereign' source to which law is so much subjected. As we saw, the modern nation state and its inflected society assume a transcendent illimitability from which a grounded affirmation cannot be derived without countering their secular pretensions. Law in its illimitability, in its vacuously 'pure' transcendence, provides that affirmation. Being dependent in this way on law's illimitability for their very constitution as distinctly modern, neither the nation state nor its society can ultimately encompass and subsume law. Hence, for example, the irresolution or absurdity, or both, attending legal 'recognition' by the sovereign state of other nation states and societies, modern or otherwise.[57]

---

[55] Peter Fitzpatrick, 'Law and Societies,' *Osgoode Hall Law Journal* 22 (1984), 115–138 and Golder and Fitzpatrick, *Foucault's Law*, chapter 2.

[56] Jacques Derrida, *Specters of Marx: The State of the Debt, The Work of Mourning, & The New International*, trans. Peggy Kamuf (New York: Routledge, 1994), xix, emphasis in the original removed.

[57] Kirsten Anker, *Declarations of Interdependence: A Legal Pluralist Approach to*

All of which poses a concluding challenge of saying what is distinct about this law, setting it apart from, as well as remaining of, society—a law that is not ultimately subsumed within or ultimately 'explained' by society empirically encased; a law that embeds possibility yet ranges still beyond it. Here the containment and sobering of law is dissipated and the sociality of law becomes a hyper-sociality. Taking a few instances almost at random, the challenge could be posed in terms of whether society could, like law, entirely create its own subjects, such as a corporation, or create entirely new modes of relation between subjects. Or one may wonder how society could, like law, create and insist on social norms that do not, or do not yet, conform to the existent state of a society. Or one may likewise wonder at law's determining of temporality, or its determining that temporality is or will be other than what it is or could be. Then there is something of a culminating instance with the 'legal fiction' in which 'the letter of the law' is sustained in its ostensible truth whilst normative effect is given to a situation quite other than that truth, this being but a stark instance of the 'fictional' quality of law, of 'fiction' inhabiting 'the very core of legal thought.'[58]

To bring matters to an end by way of the impossibility of an ending, this fictive quality is enabled by a law which, for Derrida, not only 'remains *to come*' but also 'remains *by coming*,' a 'justice' ever open to 'the coming of the other': 'it deploys the very discourse of events irreducibly to come.'[59] It has 'no horizon of expectation' and in this must be 'distinguish[ed] from the future.'[60] It is, rather, 'an imperative, necessarily present,' a response that is ever and already 'there.'[61] It is, Derrida would add with nuanced irony, a force that is a 'weakness' but a force capable of 'making the weakest strongest'; and law's insistent illimitability could add point to his concluding that 'one says to oneself, one knows that in the

---

Indigenous Rights, (Farnham: Ashgate, in press), chapter 3; Peter Fitzpatrick, 'Latin roots: the force of international law as event,' in *Events: The Force of International Law*, ed. Fleur Johns, Richard Joyce and Sundhya Pahuja (London: Routledge, 2011), 44–5.

[58] Derrida, 'Force of Law,' 240 and Jacques Derrida, 'Before the Law,' trans. Avital Ronell and Christine Roulston, in Jacques Derrida, *Acts of Literature*, (New York: Routledge, 1992), 190.

[59] Derrida, 'Force of Law,' 256, his emphasis.   [60] Derrida, 'Force of Law,' 256.

[61] Jacques Derrida, "*Pace* Not(s)", trans. John P. Leavey, in Jacques Derrida, *Parages* (Stanford: Stanford University Press, 2011), 11, 14.

end true force is on the side of the oppressed.'[62]

ENDURING THANKS to Pablo Sanges Ghetti for guidance. Much of this chapter previously emerged as a Genest Memorial Lecture at Osgoode Hall Law School on 12 March 2014. My thanks to Ruth Buchanan for the wonderful opportunity and for being supremely social.

---

[62] Jacques Derrida, 'Negotiations,' in Jacques Derrida, *Negotiations: Interventions and Interviews 1971–2001*, trans. Elizabeth Rottenberg (Stanford: Stanford University Press, 2002), 35, 36.

— 3 —

The Meaning of Sense

Pieter Meurs & Ignaas Devisch

Over the years, sense has become Nancy's master word: it pops up in almost every statement. Since the publication of *The Sense of the World*, Nancy has increasingly used sense to point to what he sees as the necessity to reinvent our ontological vocabulary in order to understand who we are and how we coexist.[1] Sense is Nancy's key to the door to the question of being. He pushes his ontological inquiry to a point where he can claim that 'being itself is given to us as sense.'[2] The question we want to tackle in this chapter is how we are to understand the implications and effects of this crucial Nancean proposition for our everyday praxis in times of globalization. For indeed, and as we will show, if Nancy's analysis of the existential condition of sense means something, it is a fundamental interpellation of our daily being-in-the-world.

The crux of our argument turns on Nancy's understanding of sense. Sense means something other than the meaning we ascribe to it in everyday life: importantly, sense differs from signification. In the short text 'The Forgetting of Philosophy,' Nancy meticulously explains signification as the establishment of the closed relation between the physical and the meta-physical.[3] Signification offers

---

[1] Jean-Luc Nancy, *The Sense of the World*, trans. Jeffrey S. Librett (Minneapolis: University of Minnesota Press, 1997).

[2] Jean-Luc Nancy, *Being Singular Plural*, trans. Robert D. Richardson and Anne E. O'Byrne (Stanford: Stanford University Press, 2000), 2.

[3] Jean-Luc Nancy, *The gravity of thought*. trans. François Raffoul and Gregory Recco (New Jersey: Humanities Press, 1997), 7–64. Originally published as Jean-Luc Nancy, *L'Oubli de la philosophie* (Paris: Galilée, 1986).

a means to represent reality and vouches for a direct and definitive equation between words and things. For example, if you are reading this text in a book, the material object lying in front of you is signified or represented by the word or concept 'book.' Nancy considers signification as a closed system, or even better, as closure itself: a book (concept) is a book (material object), not a desk or a computer. Signification objectively represents our world; it encloses or marks its limits.

On the other hand, Nancy argues that sense does not relate to a closed representation of our world, but is the infinite presentation of our world. In order to clarify his argument, Nancy refers to Heidegger's retracing of the original meaning of hermeneutics. Referring to Hermes, the Ancient Greek messenger for the Gods, Heidegger argues that hermeneutics does not so much refer to the representation or signification of a message, but rather to the messaging itself: 'hermeneuein is that exposition which brings tidings because it can listen to a message.'[4] The messenger does not interpret the message, but first of all addresses it. What is important in Heidegger's understanding of hermeneutics is the idea that a message, before anything, is not signified or interpreted, but only presents itself as such. Rather than the representation of the message, it is this presentation itself that makes up its meaning.

Nancy applies this idea of a bare messaging to his thinking of sense. Sense is not something that we know by means of representation or signification, but it is that which presents. Sense does not re-present something, but is a presenting. It addresses or touches us, before any closed representations or ideas can be made about that which is presented. In this sense, Nancy will say that sense

> has nothing to do with the recombination of—and the more or less uncertain commentary on—significations, but has everything to do with what keeps signification—either willingly or reluctantly—oscillating dangerously on its limit.[5]

Indeed, sense is what challenges our closed representations. In a way, it (re-)opens them. As such, according to Nancy, sense pre-exists signification. It is the field in which significations and representations can take place. Nancy considers sense as simultaneously the

---

[4] Martin Heidegger, *On the Way to Language*. (New York: Harper and Row Publishers Inc., 1982), 29.

[5] Nancy, *Gravity*, 67.

possibility and the limit of representation:

> The truth, this truth that our history presents to us and with which we inevitably have to do, is not that sense takes place inside and through signification, but that on the contrary, sense is the element in which there can be significations, interpretations, representations.[6]

Being (and) Sense

For Nancy, then, sense is an inappropriable element that lies beyond our words and ideas, while at the same time being the very thing that makes sense out of being: being is given to us as sense. From the moment we exist, we are confronted with sense. It is as sense that we find existence. The presentation sense implies is thus nothing other than the presentation of being. Put simply: sense = being presenting itself to us. Or, as Nancy argues: 'the there is makes sense by itself and as such.'[7]

From the idea that being is given to us as sense also follows a proposition Nancy uses in various works: we are sense. 'We' is—we are—not something that happens outside of existence. Existence happens to us; existence is us happening. Put otherwise: sense happens to us. Sense is the circulation of the being that 'we' are. Consequently, sense is not something we can 'have' (or have lost for that matter). It is not something we ascribe to the world. We are sense and there is no sense other than or outside of 'us.' Indeed, 'we are the element in which significations can be produced and circulate.'[8] As Nancy argues, this is our utmost truth: that sense takes place as 'us.' Addressing sense is addressing ourselves in our sheer existence.[9]

By considering being as sense, Nancy not only opens a general question for an understanding of ontology (being) but also asks us to deal with the very sense of our existence.[10] This is what is at stake

---

[6] Nancy, *Oubli*, 89–90 (our translation). See also Nancy, *Gravity*, 59.
[7] Nancy, *Sense of the World*, 7.   [8] Nancy, *Being Singular Plural*, 2.
[9] It is important to note here, that, engaging with Heidegger's ontological difference, Nancy differentiates between 'being as such' and 'being as being.' We hope to have made clear that sense always refers to being 'as being.' Unfortunately, there is not enough space to extensively elaborate on the internal difference of being.
[10] Van Rooden aptly summarizes Nancy's importance by making an analogy between Heidegger and Nancy: 'Similar to Heidegger, who blames philosophers for forgetting to think being which is given before beings, Nancy blames them for having forgotten to

in his philosophy: how can we address the sheer openness that we are? How can we be sensible for the sense that being is—that we are?

Sensing the World

If we understand being as sense, does this also imply a radical shift in our responsibility to the world? The clichéd question for the philosopher, 'what is the meaning of life,' presupposes an autonomous agency simply ascribing sense to the world. For Nancy, addressing sense or addressing our sheer existence does not mean that we are simply to define ourselves or the world by means of responsible, meaningful ideas and concepts. The bare existence about which he speaks lies precisely beyond such a Cartesian subject imposing its sense upon the world in order to enclose it within its meaning. We are sense refers first of all to our (f)actual being in the world, to the tangible corporeal reality of our existence. It means coming to grips with our bare being.

Since being never happens on its own, it is always already towards a world. This 'toward the world,' according to Nancy, is not a predicate, but 'the entire constitution, being, nature, essence, and identity of the absolute fragment of existence.'[11] Following Heidegger, he understands the world not simply as the space where (our) being happens, but as the taking place, the there, of being.[12] In this sense, 'being toward the world' is a tautological expression. It is truly the existential condition. '"World" says the there of the "there is."'[13] The world is the there of being, its localization or spacing.

Taking existence seriously, then, would imply that we take the world as nothing other than the to be, the happening of our existence. In order to fully grasp this existential condition of worldliness (*mondialité*), we have to examine further how Nancy understands the sense of the world. This means first of all that we should not consider it as an object 'on which one would come to confer a

think sense which is given before signification' (Aukje Van Rooden, 'L'Intrigue dénouée. Politique et littérature dans une communauté sans mythes' (PhD thesis, Universiteit van Tilburg, 2010, 111–12), our translation.

[11] Nancy, *Sense of the World*, 154.

[12] See also Pieter Meurs, 'This world without another. On Jean-Luc Nancy and *la mondialisation*,' *Journal of Critical Globalization Studies* 1 (2009), 31–46.

[13] Nancy, *Sense of the World*, 156.

sense.'[14] Indeed, the world is not an object of thought but first and foremost emerges as the taking place of being and thus of thought. It is a totality of meaning rather than something about which we can have a meaning. Nancy refers to 'world' as a whole 'to which a certain meaningful content or a certain value system properly belongs in the order of knowledge or thought as well as in that of affectivity and participation.'[15] Take for example the 'world of politics,' the 'world of sports' or the 'third world.' Each of these refers to a meaningful totality and being part of it implies a certain understanding of its content, even if it is not always made explicit as such. To appear to us as a world, one way or another we are already connected with some of its inner givens. We are already part of it; we always already share something of its meaningful content. From this follows that a world is only a world for those who inhabit it. According to Nancy, 'to inhabit' can only refer to a world. As such, it is not a space where one can be, but is the space where one takes place. By referring to the etymology of 'inhabiting'—inferring both the Latin *habere* (to be self-standing, to occupy a place, to have) and *habitus* (habit or the way in which we are)—Nancy shows the world is a *habitus* and an inhabiting. In other words: 'what takes place, takes place in a world and by way of that world.'[16] The *habitus* and habitat of the world itself, then, is nothing other than its own being. This means that the being of the world itself, stands in itself, by way of itself: it only refers to its own being. For Nancy, therefore, 'the sense of the world does not occur as a reference to something external to the world.'[17] Simply put, there cannot be an independent vantage point with relation to which the sense (or the being) of the world could be determined.

The worldliness of the world means the world can no longer have sense in reference to something outside. Today, it is however not only this loss we have to deal with, for it opens onto another contingency as well: the question for the raison d'être of the world as a totality of beings. Aside from the loss of sense, the world also seems without reason or ground. The world is not given or created, it simply is. There is no God or ultimate cause that created the world at a beginning of days. As such, it is in fact a mystery, as an

---

[14] Nancy, *Sense of the World*, 54.
[15] Jean-Luc Nancy, *The creation of the world or globalization*, trans. François Raffoul and David Pettigrew (New York: State University of New York Press, 2007), 41.
[16] Nancy, *Creation*, 42.   [17] Nancy, *Creation*, 43.

absolute fact even before and beyond its necessity or contingency. Nancy proposes to consider the world as a fact that is neither efficient nor final. The world comes before and is beyond our notions of necessity and contingency: 'to think it [the world], is to think this factuality, which implies not referring it to a sense capable of appropriating it, but to placing in it, in its truth as a fact, all possible sense.'[18] The world is, and as such it is only in and for itself. In withdrawing itself from the status of an object or signification, the world becomes nothing other than itself. It only refers to itself. As such, the world exceeds or is beyond every signification or (re)presentation. In this sense, Nancy considers 'world' as nothing other than sense. Indeed, 'world is not merely the correlative of sense; it is structured as sense, and reciprocally, sense is structured as world.'[19]

Being sensible for the sense that we are, thus means coming to grips with the very fact that we are always already thrown into a world, thrown into sense. This ontological condition is Nancy's starting point to question our metaphysical understandings of the world and it constantly reopens the question for the sense of a world. It means we can no longer fall back on a metaphysical or divine order to define the sense of our existence. As there is no originary fundament or essence of being that offers us a definite answer, in addressing the sense of being, we are exposed to ourselves and to this world.

Touching the World as Everyday Praxis

Being exposed to ourselves and to this world means that there is nothing else but us and the world. There is no subject or Subject that defines the sense of the world. There are only our bodies and our world, but this relationship transcends us, not a metaphysical transcendence stemming from another world, but as what discloses our identity onto the world. The relation between things happening in the world is constituted by the fact that their limits touch each other.

Nancy discusses the relation of touching in 'The Weight of a

---

[18] Nancy, *Creation*, 45.
[19] Nancy, *Sense of the world*, 7–8.

Thought.'[20] In this concise essay, he speaks of the touching between matter and thought. Thinking has always been conceived to be radically different to matter. According to Nancy however, thinking most certainly weighs:

> There is no doubt that meaning is incorporated (if only as a 'leap') into the reality of the real (into its matter, and thus into its weight)—just as there is no doubt that the real makes sense (it is an ideality, and therefore is without gravity).[21]

There is a relation between matter and thinking, they are (at) each other's limits. Thinking cannot be purely transparent or absolutely objective or it would make no sense at all. As such, Nancy distances himself from—what some claim to be—'Cartesian' instincts that 'lead [us] to believe that ideas must be "clear," it being understood that "clarity" is something of the order of pure transparency, perhaps even of the void.'[22] Rightfully, he questions the one who desires an empty thought: a line of thought cannot make sense on its own. On the contrary, thinking can only touch its gravity there, where there is something beyond mere thought: 'this "there" is a material point, a weighty point: the flesh of a lip, the point of a pen or of a stylus, any writing insofar as it traces out the interior and exterior edges of language.'[23]

Nancy calls this touching of thought 'ex-scription.' Ex-scription is the event where thinking comes to grips with what it tries to present or signify and what is outside itself (the thing itself, matter). It refers to the notion that thought matters (pun intended). The sense of the concept 'book,' for example, does not make sense by referring to a clean and transparent abstract category, but only insofar as it touches on the 'book' as a real thing, insofar as it has opacity, a density, or thickness. Like sense then, this is the sort of thinking that

> neither dominates nor shines down like a sun, that does not rise to the zenith, or set to the nadir, but that weighs insofar as it alights and sinks in [*s'enforce*], and even settles, each time existing here-and-now, in a singular here-and-now, and always singular anew, plurally, absolutely, as impossible to resorb as to complete.[24]

---

[20] Nancy, *Gravity*. 75–84. Originally published as Jean-Luc Nancy, *Le poids d'une pensée* (Sainte-Foy: Les Éditions le Griffon d'argile, 1991).
[21] Nancy, *Gravity*, 76.   [22] Nancy, *Gravity*, 79.   [23] Nancy, *Gravity*, 79.
[24] Nancy, *Gravity*, 82.

It is thinking that reaches beyond mere significations or words; it touches its own limit.

Consequently, touching the world is nothing other than reaching towards the limits of sense, without ever being able to appropriate it. It remains a mere touch: it implies being sensible. More concretely, it means that in thinking the sense of the world, we cannot deny the implication of this thought in that very world. It also means (b)reaching the limits of our taken-for-granted significations and representations. But this is exactly the sense of being exposed: being open towards the world. It implies the impossibility of closing off the sense of the world.

To touch thus means dismissing the possibility of an independent metaphysical place from which the world is questioned. Instead, it is the affirmation that such questioning always already happens in the world.

The Globalized World?

Where does this thought of sense bring us when it comes to the widely discussed question of globalization?[25] In *The Creation of the World or Globalization*, Nancy reminds us of the fact that our world is the only world. He describes globalization as the process by which the world gradually presents itself as the space where being takes place.[26] The process of globalization shows that the world is first of all nothing but the world, the taking place of being, and the taking place of sense. From this it follows that our understanding of the world cannot simply refer to a description or presentation of socio-economic and/or political changes. Our thinking about the world should primordially and by definition do justice to its existential condition: that it is the opening and limit of (re)presentations. Or in other words: the world is not simply something we can signify or represent, but is the essential prerequisite in order to signify or represent.

In its numerous attempts to map the sense of a global world,

---

[25] See e.g. David Held and Anthony McGrew, *Globalization/Anti-Globalization: Beyond the Great Divide* (Cambridge: Polity Press, 2007); Anthony Giddens. *Runaway World* (London: Profile Books, 2011). Zygmunt Bauman. *Globalization: The Human Consequences* (New York: Columbia University Press, 1998); Ulrich Beck, *What is globalization?* (London: Polity Press, 2000).

[26] See Nancy, *Creation*.

contemporary globalization theory fails to take this ontological stance of the world into account. It focuses on representations and significations of (changes in) the world, rather than on what the process of globalization essentially presents us: the fact that the sense of the world is first of all pure and simple praxis. The sense of a world should refer to the taking place of significations and representations rather than to a theory abstract of its place. Praxis, thus, is not to be understood as something that is opposed to theory, something that is absolutely distinct (or distant) from it. Rather, it is that in which or, as which, theory can take place. It is what opens onto theory, onto representations and significations. And as such, it is nothing other than what Nancy describes as the happening of sense. He challenges us and globalization theory to think that the sense of a global world 'is always in praxis.'[27] We cannot step outside the world to determine it objectively. The praxis of the world is something by which or through which we are. It is what determines—literally: *de-terminare*, to mark the end or limits of—our representations and significations. And as we have seen, according to Nancy, in order to touch it, we should think (at) the limits of our significations, we have to let the world speak for itself. How does this happen? How should we understand this taking place of a global world? According to Nancy, the sense of the world is something that indeed happens. It is not something that can be established as such, as something which is closed on itself. It is, as we have seen, the opening or determination of our theories and significations. This opening is an action, an event, something that happens. And it happens to us. Rather than being a determination of the world, sense first of all determines us in the way we (re)-present and signify. As such, praxis is 'an action that affects the agent, not the work.'[28] Nancy explains this effect by referring to a certain kind of passivity. He argues we should not understand this passivity as something that is opposite to activity. Passivity 'does not consist in being "passive," but in being, if we can put it this way, *passible* to meaning, that is, capable of receiving or welcoming it.'[29] What he wants to make clear, is the idea that the sense of the world as praxis is something that does happen to us, but only insofar as we are the happening. In this regard, the sense of the world understood as praxis reminds us of the idea that 'we

---

[27] Nancy, Creation, 54. [28] Nancy, *Sense of the World*, 9. [29] Nancy, *Gravity*, 69.

are sense.' It is because we are, that we bring sense into play. We are 'called to an essential and "active" relation with the proper fact of being.'[30] Consequentially, 'being' takes on an active meaning.

The ontological imperative 'we are to be' is thus rephrased into 'we are to make sense.' Nancy argues however, that this duty does not stem from a higher power or authority. Rather, it comes from being itself: being urges us to be, and this implies that we are caught up in the act of making sense.[31] This means that:

> Being, absolutely and rigorously considered as such (which also means, ... considered according to its unnominalized value as a verb—being is or exists being, it 'makes' them be, makes them make-sense), is essentially its own 'engagement' as the action of sense.[32]

According to Nancy, praxis refers to being as the engaged act of making-sense. Or, put differently: praxis refers to making-sense as the engaged act of letting being be. Consequently, the sense of the world is not a theory about or interpretation of certain events of the world. As praxis, it is the play of (the happening, the coming of) these events and their opening and limiting of theories, descriptions, significations, (re)presentations, and so on. In other words, for Nancy, it is not a matter of ascribing to the world a sense, but of entering, or rather: being entered into its sense. He plays with Marx's 11th thesis on Feuerbach here: 'The philosophers have only interpreted the world, in various ways; the point is to change it.'[33] To interpret the world, in this regard, refers to the act of simply ascribing it a signification that does not touch on its reality.

Thinking about globalization by means of Nancy's understanding of sense, impels us to focus on our engagement with the world. In other words, it refers us to the ideas and concepts that really matter to us. It reveals how we relate to the world, how we weigh into the world. This brings us back to Nancy's understanding of the touching between matter and thought: only those thoughts that touch upon the limit of sense matter. In this regard, the scholarship

---

[30] J-L Nancy, *A Finite Thinking* (Stanford: Stanford University Press, 2003), 175.

[31] However, Nancy argues no sense is being made here: 'this "making" is not a "producing"' (Nancy, *Finite*, 175). The fact that being makes sense is not a property of being. Rather, sense properly is being.

[32] Nancy, *Finite*, 177.

[33] Karl Marx and Friedrich Engels, *The German Ideology. Including Theses on Feurbach and Introduction to the Critique of Political Economy* (New York: Prometheus Books, 1998), 571.

on globalization can only 'make sense' when we approach it from where it touches us. This happens where we happen, where sense happens. But this is no place; it is the taking place of being. And as we have seen, this is nothing but the world. It is the world as world, that which is not objectively determinable or cannot be grasped by means of significations and (re)presentations. In this sense, it comes as no surprise that today there seems to be no scholarly agreement on the conceptual framework for the study of globalization.[34] This is not because the available empirical evidence is inadequate, or because the topic lacks a precise definition of its subject. Rather, it is because of the fact that the different points of view are informed by our existential condition: being and world are given to us as sense.

---

[34] See e.g. David Held, Anthony. McGrew, David. Goldblatt, and Jonathan Perraton, *Global Transformations: Politics, Economics and Culture* (Stanford: Stanford University Press, 1999); Manfred Steger, *Globalism: Market Ideology Meets Terrorism*, 2nd ed. (Oxford: Rowman & Littlefield Publishers, Inc., 2005).

Acts
of the
Social

— 4 —

Being Social Democratically with Jean-Luc Nancy at the Gezi Park Protests

Marie-Eve Morin

Nancy engages with democracy most explicitly in his little book *The Truth of Democracy*, the publication of which marks the 40th anniversary of May '68.[1] At the beginning of the eponymous essay, 'The Truth of Democracy,' Nancy identifies as the 'real singularity' of May '68 a certain disappointment with democracy itself, whose triumphal recovery after World War II failed to live up to its promises.[2] Nancy calls it a 'scarcely visible but insistent disappointment, the nagging sense that we had never recovered something whose triumphant return seemed to have been announced by the end of the Second World War, namely, democracy.'[3] The target of the May '68 uprisings was, according to Nancy, a 'kind of managerial democracy,' or what he calls elsewhere *ecotechnics*: the management of production, exchange, and growth of the world, now understood as the global *oikos*.[4] While the *polis* was supposed

---

[1] Jean-Luc Nancy, *The Truth of Democracy* (New York: Fordham University Press, 2010).   [2] Nancy, *Truth of Democracy*, 1.   [3] Nancy, *Truth of Democracy*, 4.

[4] Nancy, Truth of Democracy, 1, 49; see also Jean-Luc Nancy, *The Creation of the World* or *Globalization*, trans. François Raffoul and David Pettigrew (Albany: SUNY Press, 2007), 94.

to be the place of the production of a 'more-than-life' or a 'good life' beyond the mere satisfaction of needs, it is now reduced to a global, all-encompassing *oikos*, the management of which not only reproduces life, but also produces wealth.

The unquestioned consensus around democracy after World War II was caused, according to Nancy, less by an overall positive evaluation of democracy itself than by its evaluation in relation to 'totalitarian regimes' of all stripes. But what was obscured by this unquestioned support for democracy was the fact that the 'most significant political catastrophes' of the twentieth century, Nancy argues, 'were not the result of the sudden emergence of inexplicable demons' that were absolutely antithetical to democracy and befell it from the outside, but rather the result of an intrinsic vulnerability at the heart of democracy itself. If something makes democracy vulnerable to totalitarianism, then it is not enough to defend democracy as it now is; we must reinvent it.[5] In the few pages that follow this demand, Nancy lays down the terms of the problem and shows how such a reinvention ought to be conceived. The question had already occupied Nancy before, in the central chapters of *The Sense of the World*, in the 'complements' to *The Creation of the World*, in the essay on the Gulf War in *Being Singular Plural*, and of course, in his interventions at The Center for Philosophical Research on the Political, partially collected in *Retreating the Political*.[6] The question I would like to address in this short essay is whether Nancy's thinking of democracy can help us shed light on 'the occupations of the squares and other public spaces in early 2011.' Instead of speaking generally, I will focus on two specific events surrounding the Gezi Park protests that rocked Istanbul, and other cities in Turkey, in the weeks preceding the 'Being Social' Symposium, which took place at Birkbeck, University of London on 28 June 2013: 'the peace pianist' and 'the standing man.' I hope to hint at how Nancy's thinking of democracy, despite its ontological flavour, does indeed reanimate our thinking of praxis and resistance.

---

[5] Nancy, *Truth of Democracy*, 8

[6] Jean-Luc Nancy, *The Sense of the World*, trans. Jeffrey S. Librett (Minneapolis: University of Minnesota Press, 1997); Jean-Luc Nancy, *Being Singular Plural*, trans. Robert D. Richardson and Anne E. O'Byrne (Stanford: Stanford University Press, 2000), 101–143; Jean-Luc Nancy and Philippe Lacoue-Labarthe, *Retreating the Political*, ed. Simon Sparks (New York: Routledge, 1997).

The *demos* of democracy as singular plural

The vulnerability of democracy as Nancy diagnoses it comes from its inability to bring to light the *demos* that is supposed to be its principle.[7] Democracy is anxious to present its *demos*. Indeed, if the *demos* cannot be presented or exhibited, then what force can it have against totalitarian forces? At the same time, if democracy requires the presentation of the *demos*, the mode of its presence cannot be that of a thing or a Subject that is present in its identity with itself. Such a presentation would be exclusionary or totalitarian and would contradict the injunction of openness at the heart of democracy, since the people would then exist only as a closed totality. Derrida expresses the paradoxical nature of democracy in the following way:

> Democracy has always wanted by turns and at the same time two incompatible things: it has wanted, on the one hand, to welcome only men, and on the condition that they be citizens, brothers, and compeers [*semblables*], excluding all the others, in particular bad citizens, rogues, noncitizens, and all sorts of unlike and unrecognizable others, and, on the other hand, at the same time or by turns, it has wanted to open itself up, to offer hospitality, to all those excluded.[8]

This paradox is resolved through the process of fraternization, which allows the opening of the 'closed circle of citizens' to all, but only insofar as the foreign is first rendered similar. All are welcome, all can be citizens, provided they make themselves worthy of such belonging by imitating the true exemplar of the citizen. The role of this appeal to exemplarity ('French' as the example to be imitated to become a citizen of the *world*, or 'man' as the example to be imitated to belong to *humanity*) is to give content to the figure of the citizen, and hence to reintroduce some closure within the assertion of universality. Derrida's appeal to a 'democracy to come' then does not mean that we need to search for a democratic regime that would in the future be more inclusive or more universal insofar as its process of fraternization would

---

[7] Nancy, *Truth of Democracy*, 6; The first two sections of this paper summarize the interpretation of Nancy developed in chapter four of my book, see Marie-Eve Morin, *Jean-Luc Nancy* (Cambridge: Polity, 2012).

[8] Jacques Derrida, *Rogues: Two Essays on Reason*, trans. Pascale-Anne Brault and Michael Naas (Stanford: Stanford University Press, 2005), 63.

be more effective. Rather, it means that democracy ought to be, here and now, radically opened not only to those who imitate the exemplar but to what or who comes prior to (or regardless) of its identification as friend, as member of the family, as human being, etc. While Nancy's 'unworked community' also puts into question the possibility of a self-enclosed community, Nancy also emphasizes the danger of turning to the empty figure without content of the citizen in order to theorize the openness of community. By refusing to give content to the people, democracy leaves the way open for both totalitarianism and ecotechnics. The former reinvests the empty figure of the citizen with a content. The latter affirms the world's lack of *archē* or *telos*, but only in the form of the general equivalence of all ends and means, which becomes effective under the names of 'planetary technology' and 'world economy.'[9]

Whether democracy presents the identity of the demos by assigning it a content or resorts to a purely formal presentation under the name 'citizen,' in both cases it relies, Nancy says, on the same scheme of self-sufficiency. Nancy explains:

> In the different figures of self-sufficiency, sometimes it is the social tie itself that is self-sufficient, sometimes it is the terms or units between which the social tie passes. In both cases, ultimately the tie no longer makes up a tie, it comes undone, sometimes by fusion, sometimes by atomization.[10]

In the first case, the social bond is subsumed into a 'One,' the people, who can then easily take the place of the monarch, without radically dividing its sovereignty: the people rule as One, each rules and is ruled like any other. In the second case, the citizens are independent atoms that subsist on their own, so that the social bond becomes a superfluous addition.

What needs to be thought lies between these two options: the undoing of the social bond (as that which produces a substance or a whole) without this dissolution being felt as absence or lack, that is, without assuming that this dissolution leaves us only with untied units. Nancy's deconstruction of Christianity attempts to think nothing other.[11] It looks for a thinking of atheism that would

---

[9] Nancy, *Being Singular Plural*, 133.   [10] Nancy, *Sense of the World*, 111.

[11] See Jean-Luc Nancy, *Dis-Enclosure: The Deconstruction of Christianity*, trans. Bettina Bergo, Gabriel Malenfant, and Michael B. Smith (New York: Fordham University Press, 2008), 1–41. See also Morin, *Jean-Luc Nancy*, 48–64.

not be absentheistic, that is, it attempts to think a world without God, where the place formerly occupied by God would not be occupied by another principle—Reason, Humanity, Science, or even the Nothing—but where the transcendent place or position of the principle itself would be emptied out. Such a world would be immanent insofar as it would be without transcendent principle, but it would not be without opening. This opening would open right at the edges of the various ones that are exposed in this world and that form the multiplicity of the world.

In order to think such a 'transimmanent' world, or in order to learn to inhabit the world according to its transimmanence, what needs to be undone is the *desire* for an absolute self-sufficient foundation, or the desire for sovereignty. This undoing of sovereignty is, according to Nancy, already at work within sovereignty itself. Indeed, the theologico-political order, that is, the order in which the political totality is grounded in a transcendent principle that embodies it and presents it with its truth, wavers from within. Such a deconstruction must be differentiated from a secularization of political theology. Or it is necessary to point out that the process of secularization of the transcendent principle—sovereign is first God, then King, then the people—is not merely the transcription of a foundational logic into a secular realm, but also a process of immanentization, in which the grounding transcendence is lost.[12] At this point, the figure of the citizen displaces the concept of sovereignty by exacerbating the problem of self-foundation. The political problem is not so much anymore that of the authority of a ruler in relation to those who are ruled, an authority which in the cases of both the King and the people is derived from an absolute principle, God or Nature. Rather, it is the problem of the self-formation of an instance that is not founded on anything but itself, 'insofar as precisely, the "itself" neither precedes nor founds it but is the nothing, the very thing from which it is suspended.'[13] In a world without transcendent principle, sovereignty shatters itself in trying to found itself in nothing but itself. At the end of the theologico-political there is an opening onto the atheological, that is, for Nancy, onto our being-in-common in the world. This is why Nancy can ask, evocatively: 'What if sovereignty was the revolt of

---

[12] See Nancy, *Sense of the World*, 93 and Nancy, *Creation of the World*, 96–109.
[13] Nancy, *Creation of the World*, 103.

the people?'[14]

The notion of the singular plural that informs Nancy's work provides us with important conceptual resources to sustain the thought of a *demos* between totalization and atomization. At the same time, it is important to understand this notion in all its radicality and complexity. For Nancy, existence is necessarily in common or shared out because only a being that is not an essence immanent to itself, but is exposed to an outside, does not collapse into the black hole of immanence, but succeeds in coming to presence. To exist, to be present is to be caught in a movement of appearing between pure presence and sheer absence. Such a movement (Nancy will call it *être-à*, being unto or toward),[15] if it is to be sustained, requires a limit that separates the existent at the same time as it connects it to itself and to others. This limit, which belongs neither to the inside not to the outside, is the edge where existence happens.[16]

By affirming the singular plural character of existence then, Nancy neither posits a plurality of strict individual points, nor does he dissolve all identity into the mere indistinction of pure differences. Being singular plural means that there is always more than one singularity, but this is the case because each singularity is only what it is by being caught in an infinite process of entanglement and disentanglement with itself and with others. Since it is in this process of differentiation/identification that a singularity finds its identity, such an identity cannot consist of a fixed set of properties. It is important to underline that while the singular plural allows us to understand individuals as themselves plural, it also applies to communities. Indeed, a community is a singularity, always plural and always exposed on its limit or edge to other communities, so that it never closes itself upon itself to become a detached One. Furthermore, what Nancy says of a community also applies to the world as a whole. Any whole is for Nancy always 'a whole of articulated singularities.' Articulation here does not mean organization. It names:

> What takes place where different pieces touch each other without fusing together, where they slide, pivot, or tumble over one another,

---

[14] Nancy, *Creation of the World*, 109.   [15] Nancy, *Being Singular Plural*, 40–1.

[16] See Jean-Luc Nancy, 'Of Being-in-Common,' in *Community at Loose Ends*, ed. The Miami Theory Collective (Minneapolis: University of Minnesota Press, 1991), 3–4; Jean-Luc Nancy, The Birth to Presence, trans. Brian Holmes et al. (Stanford: Stanford University Press, 1993), 154–5.

one at the limit of the other ... without this mutual *play*—which always remains, at the same time, a play *between* them—ever forming into the substance or the higher power of a Whole. Here, *the totality is itself the play* of the articulations. This is why a whole of singularities, which is indeed a whole, does not close in around the singularities to elevate them to its power: this whole is essentially the opening of singularities in their articulations, the tracing and the pulse of their limits.[17]

Democracy, Politics, and Being-in-Common

In what way does the thought of the singular plural help us reinvent democracy by allowing us to escape the opposition between the people as a given, identifiable totality and the people as made up of detached, untied units? In *Sense of the World*, Nancy appeals to a politics of the (k)not:

> One would thus demand a politics without denouement ... a politics of the incessant tying up of singularities with each other, over each other, and through each other, without any end other than the enchainment of (k)nots, without any structure other than their interconnection or interdependence, and without any possibility of calling any single (k)not or the totality of (k)nots self-sufficient. ... Politics would henceforth be neither a substance nor a form but, first of all, a gesture.[18]

Such a politics appears to be coextensive with existence itself. Indeed, it is described in much the same terms as the movement of exposition that constitutes existence itself. Of course, for gestures of tying to be possible, certain conditions must be in place: there must be room for each and every one, 'a genuine place, one in which things can genuinely take place, where there is place for being there (in this world).'[19]

In his later works, Nancy will be much more careful to delineate the sphere of the singular plural against the sphere of the political. Nancy voices a criticism of his earlier position in an interview for the journal Vacarme in April 2000. Speaking of his 1991 essay 'La comparution: Politique à venir,' Nancy says:

---

[17] Jean-Luc Nancy, *The Inoperative Community*, ed. Peter Connor (Minneapolis: University of Minnesota Press, 1991), 76.
[18] Nancy, *Sense of the World*, 111–12.   [19] Nancy, *Creation of the World*, 42.

> I myself should have a turn at self-criticism: in writing on 'community,' on 'compearance,' then on 'being with,' I certainly think I was right to discern the importance of the motif of the 'common' and the necessity to work on it anew—but I was wrong when I thought this under the banner of 'politics.'[20]

In 'La comparution,' Nancy had equated 'politics' with the multiple and expansive presentations of the in-between. While Nancy named 'art, thought, love, glory, the body' as such presentations of the in-common, as *éclats* (shards, bursts or flashes) of sense, the role of politics was to diffract these presentations, to expose their being-in-common.[21] Politics, in this case, would be not a specific activity, but the *praxis* of sharing itself, the *praxis* that keeps open and engages the space of our multiple expositions. In this sense, politics does not assume or take over the meaning of existence as a whole; it only makes room for the sense that existents make in tying and untying themselves. Still it remains unclear in what sense politics, which is said to propagate or diffract the 'in-common,' remains distinct from the various praxes of sense it exposes.

In the *Truth of Democracy*, not only in the eponymous essay but also in the short piece 'Is Everything Political?,' Nancy is much more explicit in defining the specific role of politics in relation to the order of singular plural existence. The sense of existence, which is not a transcendent signification imposed from above, but what happens at the limit between singularities when they entangle themselves with and disentangle themselves from each other, is decided in the sphere of the in-common and not in the political sphere. At the same time, the sphere of the in-common can only be put into play in its singularity and plurality within the open space of the *polis*, even though its object proper—existence or sense—is not explicitly political. Politics, then, only gives the affirmations of singular plural existence their space and possibility;[22] it does not prefigure or determine the 'Good' of the good life that makes up political life. Instead, politics allows each and all to 'sketch out, to

---

[20] Jean-Luc Nancy, 'Nothing but the World: An Interview with *Vacarme*,' *Rethinking Marxism* 19/4 (2007), 525, translation modified.

[21] Jean-Luc Nancy, 'La Comparution/The Compearance: From the Existence of Communism to the Community of Existence,' trans. Tracy B. Strong, *Political Theory* 20/3 (1992), 390.

[22] Nancy, *Truth of Democracy*, 26.

paint, to dream, to sing, to think, to feel a "good life" that measures up incommensurably to the infinite that every 'good' envelops.'[23] Politics, Nancy says, 'is in charge of space and of spacing (of space-time), but it is not in charge of figuring.'[24] But, while the political sphere does not propose any figures, such figurelessness should not be thought of as a lack; it is rather the precondition for the proliferation of figures: works, gestures, bearings, thoughts, etc. It is for this figureless and spacious politics that Nancy reserves the name of democracy, a democracy that is essentially an-archic insofar as the *demos* does not constitute its given *archē* or principle, but represents rather what foils 'any posited, deposited, or imposed *archē*' in favour of a plurality of absolute gestures.[25]

What we have then is a complex relation between, on the one hand, the in-common as sense and democracy as the condition of possibility of the in-common, and on the other hand, the sphere of the in-common and the concrete policies that arises out of our being-together in the world. This double relation should not be understood as one of foundation. Democracy is, for Nancy, a metaphysics, not in the sense that it grounds beings as a whole in a transcendent principle, but in the sense that it ponders the being of our being-in-common, but without assuming its sense or its destination, without assuming what forms it will take.[26] Here, democracy appears to be abstract and apolitical. Indeed, it is equivalent to the thought of our being-in-common. While Nancy gives voice to this worry, he is clear that to enter into this thought at all is 'already to act. It is to be engaged in the praxis whereby what is produced is a transformed subject rather than a preformed product, an infinite subject rather than a finite object.'[27] Furthermore, this thoughtful decision in favour of being-in-common, commits us to certain 'actions, operations, and struggles' not only against the reification of being-in-common into a thingified common, but also against general equivalence.[28]

Democracy, then, constitutes the condition of possibility of a putting into play of existences. It is beyond the democratic sphere (but never apart from it) and within the sphere of being-in-common that decisions about what it means to live a 'good life' are made

---

[23] Nancy, *Truth of Democracy*, 27.   [24] Nancy, *Truth of Democracy*, 50.
[25] Nancy, *Truth of Democracy*, 31; See also Nancy, 'Of Being-in-Common,' 11.
[26] Nancy, *Truth of Democracy*, 33–4.   [27] Nancy, *Truth of Democracy*, 31.
[28] Nancy, *Truth of Democracy*, 31.

and gestures of existence are affirmed. And it is from the place of being-in-common that policies—of health, culture, or otherwise—can be devised to respond to the senses or values that are affirmed in the sphere of the in-common. But again such policies are not determined by or derived from our common existence since this existence does not form a unitotality. The two levels of politics (metaphysics/democracy and policies) are not only distinct, but each has, in its own way, being-in-common as its 'focal point.'

Gezi Park Protests: The 'Peace Pianist' and the 'Standing man'

On the evening of 12 June 2013, in the midst of protest in Istanbul and as the police and the protesters are facing off and readying themselves for another night of confrontation, a man shoves his piano up to Taksim square, near Gezi Park, right between the protesters and the police, and begins to play. *The Independent* labelled him the 'peace pianist.'[29] As *Der Spiegel* reports, people are 'magically' attracted by the sound of the music.[30] They gather around the pianist, sit down, take off the helmets they were wearing to protect themselves against stones and water cannons, and simply listen to the music, singing along. At some point in the night, the crowd around the pianist is so big that some people are almost 'sitting on the black boots of the police officers.'[31] Witnesses report a radical change in the confrontational atmosphere of the place. A relief of tension is even palpable on the side of the police. Some police officers take off their helmets and put down their shields.

It is difficult to evaluate the political significance of this event. When the *Spiegel* reporter asks Davide Martello, the pianist, what message he wanted to convey to the people on the square, he replies:

---

[29] Richard Hall, 'Turkey protests: The "peace pianist" trying to bring calm to Taksim Square,' *The Independent*, 13 June 2013, accessed 26 November 2014, http://www.independent.co.uk/news/world/europe/turkey-protests-the-peace-pianist-trying-to-bring-calm-to-taksim-square-8656968.html.

[30] Julia Jung, 'Konstanzer Pianist auf Taksim-Platz: "Die Stimmung war gigantisch",' Der Spiegel Online, accessed 26 November 2014, http://www.spiegel.de/panorama/leute/pianist-martello-spielt-auf-dem-taksim-platz-in-istanbul-a-905685.html.

[31] Matern Boeselager, 'Ausgerechnet ein deutscher Pianist rettet die Istanbuler vor dem nächsten Gasnebel,' Occupy Turkey Column, *Vice Magazine*, 13 June 2013, accessed 26 November 2014, http://www.vice.com/de/read/ausgerechnet-ein-deutschen-pianist-rettet-die-istanbuler-vor-einerm-dritten-gasnebel/.

'Talk to each other! Without spraying any gases. Stand relaxed in front of one another, drink a chai and finally begin to communicate. I played for both sides, the police and the protesters.'[32] If the goal of the performance was to prevent a violent confrontation by relieving tension and allowing both sides to enter into a rational dialogue, the most immediate effect of the performance was to silence the demands of the protesters. Indeed, Matern Boeselager reports that:

> Between the songs protesters chanted 'Taksim is everywhere, resistance is everywhere.' But when a couple of people stroke up '*Faşizme Karşı Omuz Omuza* [shoulder to shoulder against fascism],' they were brought to silence, apparently so as to not break the spell. After all police officers were standing directly besides the crowd.[33]

What is nevertheless interesting is the spatial transformation that the musical performance is able to bring about in the square. We start with a confrontational space, where two groups of people face each other along a clearly marked line. In order to prevent protesters from throwing stones at the police and triggering a violent counter-attack, some protesters move closer and form a chain in front of the police officers.[34] The location of the dividing line shifts but the spatial divide is maintained. Police officers and protesters await the event that will shift the tensed order into a violent chaos. Instead, a man positions himself right in-between the police force and the protesters, on the dividing line. What happens is a reorganization of the space: drawn by the sound of the music, the people gather in concentric circles around the man, who now represents the centre of the gathering, up until these circles reach the police officers, forcing their inclusion into the crowd of listeners. From a dual, almost Schmittian understanding of community: 'friends here, enemy there,' we seem to have switched to the unifying model of communal space criticized by Nancy: 'everybody gathered around a common cause or thing.' But if we look a little bit further, we notice

---

[32] 'Redet miteinander! Ohne irgendwelche Gase zu sprühen. Steht euch entspannter gegenüber, trinkt einen Chai und fangt endlich an zu kommunizieren. Ich habe für beide Seiten gespielt, die Polizei und die Demonstranten' (Jung, 'Konstanzer Pianist').

[33] 'Zwar wurde zwischen jedem Lied wild geklatscht und "Taksim ist überall, der Widerstand ist überall" gerufen. Aber als ein paar Leute "Schulter an Schulter gegen den Faschismus" anstimmen wollten, wurden sie von den anderen zum Schweigen gebracht, anscheinend, um den Zauber nicht zu brechen, schließlich standen die Polizisten direkt dabei' (Boeselager, 'Ausgerechnet ein deutscher Pianist').

[34] Boeselager, 'Ausgerechnet ein deutscher Pianist.'

that the dissolution of the tensions between police and protesters, even though it required a moment of unification, allowed for the re-emergence of being-in-common, of a singular plural public space. At the end of the night, Boeselager reports that 'the ferocious warriors have transformed themselves into carefree young people again.' Protestors are walking around in small groups, talking and laughing; some police officers are talking with protesters, and once in a while, some of them even smile; a group of people are dancing on one side; others are playing soccer.[35] This transformation can be seen as the, certainly limited and fleeting, political success of this particular event, since the protests first targeted a decision of the Erdogan government to turn a public space, the Gezi Park, into a privately owned shopping centre.

A couple of days after the performance by the peace pianist, Taksim Square had been forcefully cleared, closed, and finally reopened to the public, but any kind of public gatherings on the square were banned. Then, a man walked up to the Atatürk Cultural Centre in Taksim Square and stood silently for hours while he gazed straight at the portrait of Atatürk.[36] The man was performance artist Erdem Gündüz and his performance became famous as 'the standing man.' Standing there alone, he cannot be said to be part of a gathering. As others came and stood with him, questions arise: Are these people standing together? What kind of community is this? Is it a gathering or not, and are the police entitled to dismantle the 'group'? In fact, after others joined Gündüz in his silent and still protest, the police watched for a while, but then moved in and dismantled what they considered to be a gathering, arresting some of its participants. The next day, the standing man's performance caught on. The *Hürriyet Daily* reports that:

[35] 'Die Demonstranten liefen in Grüppchen umher und lachten, aus den grimmigen Kriegern waren wieder sorglose Jugendliche geworden. Die Polizisten hatten die Schilde und Helme abgelegt und sich auf den Boden gesetzt. An der Statue standen sie im Kreis, umringt von Demonstranten, mit denen sie diskutierten oder sogar einfach schwatzten, immer öfter lächelte sogar der ein oder andere. Auf der anderen Seite hatte sich eine Tanzgruppe vor dem mittlerweile ausgeschalteten Wasserwerfer gebildet, davor spielten ein paar Jungs Fußball.' (Boeselager, 'Ausgerechnet ein deutscher Pianist').

[36] Karim Talbi, 'Turkey's "Standing Man" Protest By Erdem Gunduz Spreads Across Country,' *Huffington Post*, 18 June 2013, accessed 26 November 2014 http://www.huffingtonpost.com/2013/06/18/turkey-standing-man-protest-erdem-gunduz_n_3458390.html; '"Standing man" sparks a static social revolution,' *The Newcastle Herald*, 21 June 2013, accessed 26 November 2013, http://www.theherald.com.au/story/1589022/standing-man-sparks-a-static-social-revolution/?cs=12.

Many men and women inspired by Gündüz's solo protest have held similar protests in several cities including Istanbul, Ankara and İzmir since then. Some read books while standing, others held a sit-in protest and one man dressed in a traditional costume. Some stand for hours, some for a few minutes, but these new silent protests seem to be the new phenomenon of the Gezi Park protests.[37]

The reaction of Deputy Prime Minister Bülent Arınç to this silent resistance is quite telling. He calls the protest 'pleasing to the eye' and 'civilized,' and affirms that since they are not acts of violence, such protests cannot be condemned.[38] At the same time, he worries about traffic disturbances, the health impact of standing for extended periods of time, and finally the loss of productivity: 'We should encourage such protests within the law,' says Arınç, 'However, I think they should stand for five minutes and then go to their work or school in the sixth minute. Eight hours is too long.'[39] Unable to subsume these 'standing' protests under the category of 'political protests' because of the features they display (non-violent, aesthetically pleasing, civilized), Arınç cannot condemn them. Lacking arguments against them at the political level, he resorts to other categories: health, work, traffic. 'Useless' activities, such as standing in the middle of a public square reading a book, can be tolerated, but they should not interfere with productive, goal-oriented everyday life.

When asked about the meaning of his action, Gündüz does not actually state any specific message, but rather emphasizes the importance of the idea of silent resistance and says that he hopes 'people stop and think, "what happened there?"' Gündüz does not hold a placard, does not chant.[40] Remaining silent, he cannot be

---

[37] 'Group stands against "standing man" in Istanbul protest square,' *Hürriyet Daily News*, 19 June 2013, accessed 26 November 2014, http://www.hurriyetdailynews.com/group-stands-against-standing-man-in-istanbul-protest-square.aspx?pageID=238&nID=49111&NewsCatID=341.

[38] Majid Mohamed, 'Turkey unrest: "Standing Man" inspires hundreds with silent vigil in Taksim Square,' *The Independent*, 19 June 2013, accessed 26 November 2014, http://www.independent.co.uk/news/world/europe/turkey-unrest-standing-man-inspires-hundreds-with-silent-vigil-in-taksim-square-8663201.html; '"Standing man" sparks a static social revolution;' Mohamed, 'Turkey unrest.'

[39] Cited in '"Standing man" sparks a static social revolution.'

[40] '"Standing man" inspires Turkish protesters in Istanbul,' *BBC News*, 18 June 2013, accessed 26 November 2014, http://www.bbc.co.uk/news/world-europe-22949632.

seen as raising any demands. Rather, he comes to presence in the public space, exposing himself as this singularity that he is, and his presentation remains without transcendent signification. Nancy would say, he opens up a place or spaces out the 'there' to receive his presence. If others join in it cannot be because they share the same demands. While Gündüz's performance might appear individualistic, almost atomistic, it does give rise to a sort of gathering, but not one that is unified around a common demand or cause. The participants do not even gaze in the same direction. Rather, they come and stand only in order to present themselves there too: *with* him, but also beside and apart from him. What is being enacted is the presentation of their naked being-in-common.

In an article published in *The Independent*, Kerem Nisancioglu criticized the importance given by the media to Gündüz's action and to the 'standing protests' in general. He recognizes that 'the standing man served to expose the dangerous absurdity of state violence currently taking place in Turkey,' since it led to many being arrested for doing quite literally nothing.[41] At the same time, he deplores the fact that these events have obscured other, politically more potent, developments within the protest movement. Indeed, Nisancioglu argues that the closure of Gezi Park for gatherings and demonstration was a blessing in disguise since it led people to gather spontaneously at other parks around Istanbul, where they held discussions about the future of the movement. These forums, he writes,

> are nothing short of remarkable—prefigurative spaces in which people are experimenting with, and cultivating, new, more extensive, more direct forms of democracy. Drawing on procedures common to the Indignados and Occupy movements, consensus decision making and horizontal organization forms are taking root.[42]

In these forums, public space is reclaimed by citizens against the authoritarian power of the state. Since such local organizations are not bound to a symbolic place like the Gezi Park or the Zuccotti Park, but can gather spontaneously anywhere, and since they are

---

[41] Kerem Nisancioglu, 'Turkey's "Standing Man" captured attention, but protest doesn't stand still—it forms assemblies,' *The Independent*, 25 June 2013, accessed 26 November 2014, http://www.independent.co.uk/voices/comment/turkeys-standing-man-captured-attention-but-protest-doesnt-stand-still--it-forms-assemblies-8672456.html.

[42] Kerem Nisancioglu, 'Turkey's "Standing Man" captured attention.'

not tied to specific demands and objectives, but are opened to discussions about various demands and actions, they cannot be so easily contained and repressed by state power. Indeed, these local, non-hierarchical community organizations are experiments in direct democracy, in *real* democracy, 'against the subverted nature of representative capitalist democracy.'[43]

If we remember what Nancy says about democracy being the condition of possibility of the exercise of our being-in-common, then the performance of the standing man appears not so much as distraction from these participatory forums, but rather as the political gesture underlying them. If democracy is first a metaphysics, the thought of our being-in-common, before being a way of organizing ourselves politically in order to debate and decide about the content of the good life, then the standing man can be seen as enacting this thought, and through this enactment as opening up the democratic sphere. The performance of the standing man makes possible the participatory, non-hierarchical forums where the meaning of our being-in-common can be debated democratically. By that I am not claiming that Gündüz needed to stand on Taksim Square before people could assemble at various parks throughout the city. Such a claim would be absurd. But in each citizen who attends these forums, we need to recognize the gesture of standing men or women: the presentation of a singularity, the coming to presence of a singular existence. Only this gesture can maintain the singular plurality and plural singularity of the democratic space in which debates and decisions will take place.

---

[43] Jerome Roos, 'Assemblies emerging in Turkey: a lesson in democracy,' *Roar Magazine*, 19 June 2013, accessed 26 November 2014, http://roarmag.org/2013/06/assemblies-emerging-in-turkey-a-lesson-in-democracy/.

— 5 —

The Queer Experience of Singular Finitude

Tara Mulqueen

At the end of *The Unavowable Community*, Maurice Blanchot issues what can be read as a political directive: we must seek out 'new relationships, always threatened, always hoped for, between what we call work, *oeuvre*, and what we call unworking, *désoeuvrement*.'[1] The question comes after an extended reflection on the unavowable or what Jean-Luc Nancy refers to as the inoperative.[2] The inoperative or the unavowable, the unworking, is our sociality as such—the necessarily shared experience of singular finitude in birth and death which is the irrevocable basis of sociality. The inoperative expresses precisely that which cannot be grasped; it is 'that which, before or beyond the work, withdraws from the work, and which, no longer having to do either with production or with completion, encounters interruption, fragmentation, suspension.'[3] For Blanchot, the unavowable similarly refers to 'a world which is ours for being nobody's.'[4] The inoperative is that which

---

[1] Maurice Blanchot, *The Unavowable Community* (Barrytown: Station Hill Press, 1988), 56.

[2] The inoperative and the unavowable are not precisely interchangeable, but express competing readings of Georges Bataille by Nancy and Blanchot, respectively. The basis of their disagreement will not be pursued here. For a good summary, see Ian James, *The Fragmentary Demand: An Introduction to the Philosophy of Jean-Luc Nancy* (Stanford: Stanford University Press, 2006), 187–93. Notably, however, Nancy acknowledges and accepts Blanchot's criticism, see Jean-Luc Nancy, 'Confronted Community,' *Postcolonial Studies* 6/1 (2003), 23–36.

[3] Jean-Luc Nancy, *Inoperative Community* (Minneapolis: University of Minnesota Press, 1991), 31.

[4] Blanchot, *Unavowable*, 29.

exceeds and even confounds discursive knowledge; it cannot be contained within it. For in the moment the inoperative is grasped or made into a work, avowed or claimed for some project, it becomes operative, and becomes something else, leaving the inoperative in its workless activity.

It is thus not easy to respond to Blanchot's call. He himself expresses a fondness for the events of May '68, yet that was only a fleeting political moment. Perhaps these relationships can only ever be fleeting: the 'new relationships' he seeks are threatened by their own tendency toward an (ultimately unattainable) immanence, not to mention movements from outside which would seek to appropriate and subordinate less determinative modes of relationality. As exemplified by his own strategies of writing, what is sought by Blanchot is a politics, a relationality, which would subsist between the work and the unworking, and in so doing, consistently undermine its own tendency toward absolutism. Queer politics, as they emerged in the 1980s and 1990s, can be read as a possible response to Blanchot, as an instancing of the relationality he seeks which would move beyond the realm of writing and literature; to address other modalities of being in relation with others, modalities which are perhaps more conventionally regarded as political.[5] Counterintuitively, this political modality is exposed and emerges through the experience of death.

In queer's affirmative disavowal of categories of identity, particularly when confronted with the experience of death and threat of physical violence during the AIDS epidemic, there emerges a profoundly affirmative politics which paradoxically negates and unworks categories of identity. This is not to present queer as an ideal political modality—it is as vulnerable to totalizing tendencies as anything else—but rather to reflect on a particular historical moment and to consider why the experience of death created this politics which had as its aim the rupture of categories. Death is the 'origin of possibility' but also that which is radically impossible and escapes determination.[6] With the queer experience of singular finitude, queer is read as an expression of singular finitude; concomitantly, the experience of singular finitude is thought to

---

[5] That said, 'writing' as understood by both Blanchot and Nancy would equally apply to these 'other' modalities. See ch. 8.

[6] Maurice Blanchot, *The Space of Literature* (Lincoln: University of Nebraska Press, 1982), 239.

be quintessentially queer. In pursuing this connection between the inoperative or the unavowable and queer, I hope to give some indication as to how 'the political' of poststructuralist thought might be seen at play in the world through queer politics of the early 1990s.

Being Queer

One of the first non-derogatory usages of the term queer, to designate a kind of interstitial and consequently marginalized form of existence is by Gloria Anzaldua in the 1981 collection *This Bridge Called My Back*. She was reflecting on the experiences of exclusion among lesbian women of colour when she wrote: '[w]e are the queer groups, the people that don't belong anywhere... and because we do not fit we are a threat.'[7] Lesbian women of colour crossed too many boundaries; they confounded categories through their presence at an intersection of race, gender and sexual oppression. The frustration expressed by Anzaldua was in part a consequence of the strict identity politics practiced by the gay movement at the time—and indeed, still characterizes the contemporary mainstream Lesbian, Gay, Bisexual and Transgender (LGBT) movement in many ways. These politics did not challenge practices of categorization themselves, but often reinforced categorical boundaries through a more or less liberal demand for political recognition and equal entitlement to civil rights for those designated by the respective identities. They 'responded... within the logic of the system by producing, according to the existing rules of inquiry, a truth of themselves different from the prejudicial stereotypes that justified discrimination against them.'[8] This truth was asserted in the form of coherent and essentialized identities which, it could then be argued, deserved recognition just like any other. Those who could not be easily reconciled to these categories or who experienced overlapping forms of oppression were subject to marginalization within and exclusion from these movements. Being queer, Anzaldua

---

[7] Gloria Anzaldua, 'La Prieta,' in *This Bridge Called My Back: Writings from Radical Women of Color*, ed. Gloria Anzaldua and Cherrie Moraga (New York: Kitchen Table, Women of Color Press, 1981), 232. Robert McRuer claims that Anzaldua was the first to use the term 'queer' in this way; see Robert Mcruer, 'Review of Genealogy of Queer Theory,' *NWSA Journal* 14/2 (2002) 227–9.

[8] William Turner, *A Genealogy of Queer Theory* (Philadelphia: Temple University Press, 2000), 16.

tells us, means not fitting.

Queer emerges more prominently in the early nineties, at the height of the AIDS epidemic. Before it was taken up academically, it was a politics of the street, having been appropriated by a direct action group in New York City called Queer Nation. In the manifestos of Queer Nation, there is an unabashed anger and a clear acknowledgment that the struggle of queers exceeds any kind of call for equal rights:

> How can I tell you. How can I convince you, brother, sister, that your life is in danger: That everyday you wake up, alive, relatively happy, functioning human being, you are committing a rebellious act. You as an alive and functioning queer are a revolutionary.[9]

Queer politics are, in this iteration, concerned with life and death, emphasizing that the mere existence of queers as unruly, non-conforming, and incomprehensible beings, echoing Anzaldua, constitutes a threat to the system and the status quo and endangers their own lives in turn.

It is a threat that Queer Nation sought to amplify through direct action. Rather than seeking conformity and inclusion, these direct actions pursued rupture. Queer Nation's tactics, such as invading straight bars for a 'Queer Night Out' or staging kiss-ins demonstrated a hyperbolic disregard for identity politics and the liberal rights framework.[10] These actions were also aggressively affirmative of queer being, exposing the queer margins of heteronormative society. Berlant and Freeman describe these as 'militant-erotic interventions'

> in which an official space such as a city plaza is transfused with the juices of unofficial enjoyment: embarrassment, pleasure, spectacle,

---

[9] Anonymous, 'Queers Read This,' (June 1990), accessed 11 October 2012, http://www.actupny.org/documents/QueersReadThis.pdf.

[10] Judith Butler provides the following analysis: 'Mobilized by the injuries of homophobia, theatrical rage reiterates those injuries precisely through an 'acting out,' one that does not merely repeat or recite those injuries, but that also deploys a hyperbolic display of death an injury to overwhelm the epistemic resistance to AIDS and the graphics of suffering, or a hyperbolic display of kissing to shatter the epistemic blindness to an increasingly graphic and public homosexuality' (Judith Butler, *Bodies That Matter* [Abingdon: Routledge, 1993], 178). For a good overview of Queer Nation's tactics and sometimes paradoxical approaches, see Lauren Berlant and Elizabeth Freeman, 'Queer Nationality,' *Fear of a Queer Planet: Queer Politics and Social Theory*, ed. Michael Warner (Minneapolis: University of Minnesota Press, 1993), 193–229.

longing, and accusation interarticulate to produce a public scandal that is ... Queer Nation's specialty.[11]

Part and parcel with this, there was also a distinct recognition of the danger of homophobia and the daily violence committed against people within the LGBT community, as well as the violence effected by the AIDS epidemic. As the manifesto recounts, '[e]very day one of us is taken by the enemy. Whether it's an AIDS death due to homophobic government inaction or a lesbian-bashing in an all-night diner (in a supposedly lesbian neighbourhood).'[12] The activities of Queer Nation groups such as the Pink Panthers, who patrolled streets in small troupes, confronted this violence directly.[13]

In her book *Tendencies*, Eve Kosofsky Sedgwick gives a brief etymology of the word queer. She writes that 'queer is a continuing moment, movement, motive—recurrent, eddying, *troublant*. The word 'queer' itself means *across*.'[14] Queer is meant, in this sense, as a gesture or an act of cutting across, and thereby destabilizing, modes of categorization. Drawing on Foucault, queer also expresses the contention that sexuality is an historical concept: the very idea that an individual could have a discrete sexual identity is a construct, rather than an essential truth. Organizing and researching along those lines or trying to liberate an otherwise repressed sexuality merely reinforces the myth that sexuality exists prior to its repression. Queer works to confound these categories, demonstrate their incoherence, and promulgate a 'fundamental reconceptualization of the political, beginning with our understanding of individual identity as the foundation of political organization and action.'[15]

In its academic usage, queer theory emerges from the feminist movement, from a need to deconstruct the category of 'woman.'[16] In

---

[11] Berlant and Freeman, 'Queer Nationality,' 208.

[12] Anonymous, 'Queers Read This,'

[13] Berlant and Freeman, 'Queer Nationality,' 208.

[14] Eve Kosofsky Sedgwick, *Tendencies* (London: Routledge, 1994), xii. The rallying cry of the enraged queer on the streets and queer in the academy are not as disparate as one might imagine. Academically, queer theory is most often said to have been inaugurated with the work of Judith Butler and Eve Kosofsky Sedgwick, among others, heavily influenced by Foucault's *History of Sexuality Vol. 1* and poststructuralism more generally.

[15] Turner, *Genealogy*, 3.

[16] Turner, *Genealogy*, 5. However, the relationship between feminism and queer is subject to debate and can be considered variously analogous and overlapping and at other times clearly divided. See, for instance, Henry Abelove, Michele Aina Barale and

Gender Trouble, Butler asks '[i]s the construction of the category of women as a coherent and stable subject an unwitting regulation and reification of gender relations?'[17] Anzaldua confronts precisely this problem in attempting to gain recognition for the overlapping and intersectional forms of oppression experienced by lesbian women of colour. 'What am I?' she asks. '*A third world lesbian feminist with Marxist and mystic leanings.* They would chop me up in little fragments and tag each piece with a label.'[18] But then, she cuts to the point, and exemplifies the unworking of categories performed by queer: 'Who me, confused? Ambivalent? No. Only your labels split me.'[19] Similar to the Queer Nation manifesto, which suggests that the most rebellious act is simply living, Anzaldua's response reads as an affirmation of life in excess of any particular category.[20]

Being Social

This excess lived and affirmed by Anzaluda and Queer Nation is an excess which accompanies all singularity. To the extent that categories of identity would purport to be able to completely determine being and definitively express what one *is*, in reality, as Nancy explains, '[e]very *one* displaces or disarranges sovereignty and community.' This operation of displacement or disarrangement of immanent communities and sovereign formations is not the operation of an essential individuality, but precisely the opposite:

David M. Halperin, introduction to *The Lesbian and Gay Studies Reader* (New York, Routledge, 1993), xv.

[17] Judith Butler, *Gender Trouble: Feminism and the Subversion of Identity* (New York: Routledge, 1990, 1999), 7.

[18] Anzaldua, 'La Prieta,' 228; her emphasis.   [19] Anzaldua, 'La Prieta,' 228.

[20] There is also some need to maintain a sense of the word queer which is distinct from any particular institutional context. As Nikki Sullivan summarizes: 'While Queer Theory may now be recognized by many as an academic discipline, it nevertheless continues to struggle against the straitjacketing effects of institutionalization, to resist closure and remain in the process of ambiguous (un)becoming.' (Nikki Sullivan, *A Critical Introduction to Queer Theory* (New York: New York University Press, 2003)). It is the very ambiguity of the term, and the extent to which it cannot be pinned down or easily defined, which animates queer. With this, there is a concerted effort to focus on action and praxis, not definition—to think about what queer *does* as opposed to what it *is*. While susceptible to the same kinds of totalizing and exclusionary tendencies as anything else, queer is not just a word used to describe a way of being in the world or an umbrella term for non-normative expressions of gender and sexuality, it is an action, the disruption of particular categories of identity and of processes of categorization themselves.

singular finitude.[21] The notion of singular finitude, or the shared finitude of death, goes to the heart of Nancy's notion of inoperative community. Perhaps counterintuitively, in this reading, death or finitude is not that which would reaffirm an ultimate individuality, but rather, it is that which is most fundamentally shared. It is that which establishes a necessary sociality, a fundamental sharing which prevents any kind of pure separation, such as that which would be required to establish an identity category.

The inoperative community, as presented above, is how Nancy refers to a fundamental, originary sociality.[22] It is the fact that prior to all determination, we are always-already in common with one another. And it is this very commonality, our originary sociality, which simultaneously makes possible and undermines determination. This sociality is constantly creating new relationships which exceed the categories used to determine and make sense of the world, such that one can never truly 'fit' into a category. And this is so precisely because of death. While Nancy dismisses certain aspects of Georges Bataille's engagement with community, claiming that he was never able to arrive at a sense of community which 'would open up, in and of itself, at the heart of being-in-common,' what Nancy does accept is that death is the fundamental experience of community.[23] As Ian James explains, '[d]eath, then, in Bataille's terms is not something which can be thought in isolation from community, indeed it is on the basis of the fact that our mortality or finitude is always already shared that community can exist in the first instance.'[24]

Thus, rather than singular finitude expressing a sense of individuality through mortality, it is precisely this finitude which irrevocably attaches us to community. As Nancy explains, '[s]haring comes down to this: what community reveals to me, in presenting to me my birth and my death, is my existence outside myself.'[25] Singular being is finite being—it is temporally and spatially limited— but that finitude is entirely dependent upon community as 'only the community can present me my birth, and along with it the impossibility of my reliving it, as well as the impossibility of my crossing

---

[21] Jean-Luc Nancy, *Sense of the World* (Minneapolis: University of Minnesota Press, 1997), 114.
[22] Nancy, *Inoperative*, 28. [23] Nancy, *Inoperative*, 21.
[24] James, *Fragmentary*, 18. [25] Nancy, *Inoperative*, 26.

over into my death.'²⁶ We do not experience our own birth or death; rather, it is experienced in and through community, always by others. Blanchot explains that '[t]his is what founds community. There could not be a community without the sharing of that first and last event which in everyone ceases to be able to be just that (birth, death).'²⁷ Even one who would find themselves completely alone experiences this isolation only as a result of their already being in community.

The experience of singular finitude, that which founds community, is itself the very source of inoperativity because finitude cannot be employed for any end, but rather contains its own end.²⁸ The singularity which is exposed by community is not a work or the end result of any process: '[s]ingularity perhaps does not *proceed* from anything. It is not a work resulting from an operation.'²⁹ Moreover, Nancy claims that it is 'impossible to *make a work*' of death.³⁰ This is perhaps a more controversial claim that the foregoing one. Surely, death is appropriated for all manner of political programmes, among them the deepest forms of nationalism. The power to deal out death is also one which every legal system has at its disposal in one way or another. Indeed, in the context of the AIDS epidemic, while death from disease was taking away loved ones, simultaneously the state wielded death, via exclusion and marginalization, against those very communities.

Yet Nancy maintains, echoing Bataille, that death is useless excess—it can be made to serve no purpose. No matter how death is used, that same death will ultimately undermine every attempt at absolute immanence. This is because absolute immanence *is* death: '[t]he fully realized person of individualistic or communistic humanism is the dead person. In other words, death, in such a community, is not the unmasterable excess of finitude, but the infinite fulfillment of an immanent life: it is death itself consigned to immanence.'³¹ This pursuit of absolute immanence results in death, which escapes projects and programmes.

> Death is an experience that a collectivity cannot make its *work* or its property, in the sense of something that would find its meaning in a value or cause transcending the individual. A society may well

---

²⁶ Nancy, *Inoperative*, 15.   ²⁷ Blanchot, *Unavowable*, 9.   ²⁸ Nancy, *Sense*, 32.
²⁹ Nancy, *Inoperative*, 27.   ³⁰ Nancy, *Inoperative*, 15; his emphasis.
³¹ Nancy, *Inoperative*, 13.

use it (in the celebrations of heroes or the sacrificial victims), but there is a point at which death exposes a radical meaninglessness that cannot be subsumed. And when death presents itself as *not ours*, the very impossibility of representing its meaning spends or breaches the possibility of self-presentation and exposes us to our finitude.[32]

This exposure to finitude is exposure to community, to sociality. Finitude itself is not something which can be grasped, 'finitude itself *is* nothing; it is neither a ground, nor an essence, nor a substance.'[33] Inoperative community is the very exposition of finitude.[34] A community, in the inoperative sense, 'is the presentation to its members of their mortal truth.'[35] Concomitantly, it is because of death or finitude that community as such is impossible.

Death or finitude, in this sense, is what carries the subject outside of itself; it 'irremediably exceeds the resources of a metaphysics of the subject.'[36] It is the experience of being present for the death of another which would call the self into question:

> To remain present in the proximity of another who by dying removes himself definitively, to take upon myself another's death as the only death that concerns me, this is what puts me beside myself, this is the only separation that can open me, in its very impossibility, to the Openness of a community.[37]

This proximity is an important differentiation between death which would be instrumentalized for a programme in the attempt to forge a unity (i.e. the nation) and the experience of death which is ruptural and exposes community. This is one way, I propose, to understand the political effect of the AIDS epidemic, an exposure of the political, and the emergence of queer politics, to which I turn now.

The Queer Experience of Singular Finitude

The queer experience of singular finitude recalls the immediate context in which queer politics emerged at the height of the AIDS epidemic.[38] As recounted earlier, the reappropriation of the word

---

[32] Christopher Fynsk, 'Forward' to *Inoperative Community*, by Jean-Luc Nancy (Minnesota: University of Minnesota Press: 1991), xvi.

[33] Nancy, *Inoperative*, 28.   [34] Nancy, *Inoperative*, 26.   [35] Nancy, *Inoperative*, 15.

[36] Nancy, *Inoperative*, 14.   [37] Blanchot, *Unavowable*, 9.

[38] For an excellent analysis of the affective politics of the organization ACT UP and

queer, from a term of derision and suspicion to its inverse, came in part as an expression of frustration with the gay and lesbian movement and its emphasis on categories of identity, which came to be seen as not only divisive, but also complicit in the replication of the very modes of oppression which the gay liberation movement sought to resist. Motivating this was the daily hardship of the AIDS epidemic and a sense that categories of identity were unable to provide any protection from the unyielding spread of the disease: 'queer activism's necessity and urgency lay in its challenge to the notion that identities could classify people, keep people safe, and keep them alive.'[39] It was imperative to make clear that while the majority of those affected were gay men, it was not *because* of gayness that they had contracted disease—and the same for the other marginalized populations who bore the brunt of the epidemic.

The immediate experience of death (primarily) in the gay community, when friends and loved ones were dying in great numbers for reasons that were still barely understood, created the impetus to articulate and practice a queer politics not only as a harsh and necessary turn to the physicality and mortality of the body, but also as a movement away from any fixation on individual identity or essence. The following excerpt from one of the Queer Nation manifestos is indicative of this:

> I'm reminded of the people who strip and stand before a mirror each night before they go to bed and search their bodies for any mark that might not have been there yesterday. A mark that this scourge has visited them. And I'm angry when the newspapers call us 'victims' and sound alarms that 'it' might soon spread to the 'general population.' And I want to scream 'Who the fuck am I?' And I want to scream at New York Hospital with its yellow plastic bags marked 'isolation linen,' 'ropa infecciosa' and its orderlies in latex gloves and surgical masks skirting the bed as if its occupant will suddenly leap out and douse them with blood and semen giving them too the plague. And I'm angry at straight people who sit smugly wrapped in their self-protective coat of monogamy and heterosexuality confident that this disease has nothing to do with

---

the emergence of the queer movement, see Deborah B. Gould, *Moving Politics: Emotion and Act Up's Fight Against AIDS* (Chicago: University of Chicago Press, 2009).

[39] Iain Morland and Anna Willox, introduction to *Queer Theory* (New York: Palgrave Macmillan, 2005), 2.

them because 'it' only happens to 'them.'[40]

This experience of death, and denial by heteronormative society, functions as Blanchot describes in a reflection on Bataille: 'death, the death of the other, like friendship or love, clears the space of intimacy or interiority which is never (for Georges Bataille) the space of a subject, but a gliding beyond limits.'[41] Screaming 'who the fuck am I?' can be read, in all of its anger, as a call for communication, and as a demand to break down the 'us' and the 'them' which constituted the relationship between heterosexual and homosexual worlds. The categories of identity broke down when confronted with death which superseded them.

However, it was not just the death caused by AIDS which sparked the queer movement, it was compounded by the violence enacted against people with AIDS which prompted this angry, ruptural political response, as the excerpt above suggests. The AIDS epidemic in many ways only exacerbated the violence of the division between hetero- and homosexual, as the occasion of the epidemic warranted the radical exclusion of homosexuals and particularly those suspected of having HIV or AIDS.[42]

> Doctors have refused to operate on people known to be infected with the HIV virus, schools have forbidden children with AIDS to attend classes, and recently citizens of the idyllically named town of Arcadia, Florida, set fire to the house of a family with three hemophiliac children apparently infected with HIV.[43]

Moreover, the concern of states (UK and USA notably) was much more with preventing the spread of the disease among mainstream populations, for instance, through the use of condoms among heterosexual couples, than with preventing and treating the disease amongst those who were worst effected and most vulnerable. Queer manifests anger in response to this while also dissolving divisions amongst gays and lesbians.

> When a lot of lesbians and gay men wake up in the morning we feel angry and disgusted, not gay. So we've chosen to call ourselves

---

[40] Anonymous, 'Queers Read This.' [41] Blanchot, *Unavowable Community*, 16.
[42] Leo Bersani, 'Is the Rectum a Grave?,' *October* 43 (1987), 199.
[43] Bersani, 'Is the Rectum a Grave?,' 199.

> queer. Using 'queer' is a way of reminding us how we are perceived by the rest of the world. It's a way of telling ourselves we don't have to be witty and charming people who keep our lives discreet and marginalized in the straight world. We use queer as gay men loving lesbians and lesbians loving being queer. Queer, unlike GAY, doesn't mean MALE. And when spoken to other gays and lesbians it's a way of suggesting we close ranks, and forget (temporarily) our individual differences because we face a more insidious common enemy. Yeah, QUEER can be a rough word but it is also a sly and ironic weapon we can steal from the homophobe's hands and use against him.[44]

And yet, perhaps surprisingly, the politics which emerged from this anger was the dramatically, hyperbolically affirmative queer politics described above: invading straight bars, hosting kiss-ins. While negating categories of identity, queer also affirmed the excess of life beyond those categories and, in their confrontational resistance, fought back against the instrumentalization of death against them, death as eradication; it is in one sense, a battle of one death, death as principle, and another, death as instrument, against each other.

For Nancy, it is the immediate experience of death, as the exposure of community, which creates 'the possibility of the political.'[45] Queer consists in this exposure of community rather than its presupposition and thus might be understood as 'a politics that does not stem from the will to realize an essence.'[46] The response to this experience of death was to articulate a politics based not on identity but on practice, upon a commonality that no longer assumed a common being, but rather a being-in-common. The scarring experience of death is generative: the result of this experience is the creation or opening up of 'new ways of doing politics.'[47] As indicated earlier, queer here is taken to be an expression of inoperativity or a way of engaging with or accessing the inoperative. For Nancy, inoperativity comes with an 'irrepressible political exigency'; it is an 'infinite resistance' as it never stops occurring; the unworking is constant, and as the queer experience clearly demonstrates, it is lived.[48] I put forward that queer can be conceived of as a 'new relationship' between the operative and the inoperative: that queer, in its status as a doing and a constant unworking of identity without any fixed or determinate horizon,

[44] Anonymous, 'Queers Read This.'
[45] Nancy, *Inoperative*, xxxviii.   [46] Nancy, *Inoperative*, xl.
[47] Walters, 'From Here to Queer,' 6.   [48] Nancy, *Inoperative*, 80.

is in itself a praxis, a discourse of inoperativity.[49] 'Queer is by definition whatever is at odds with the normal, the legitimate, the dominant. There is nothing in particular to which it necessarily refers. It is an identity without an essence.'[50] Queer, in its inability to be placed, to be substantively defined, and its propensity to be that which is always strange and always against the normative, reflects this infinite resistance. The being of queer, which is a doing, is constantly unworking any fixed or circumscribed identity.

Queer serves as an example of this infinite resistance, but also, I would argue, adds something to it. For those who would claim that inoperativity, like deconstruction, leaves no room for political decisiveness or action, queer becomes a way of engaging the *activity* of inoperativity, an act of interruption.[51] Queer, however, is not presented as being beyond this essential problematic of the subject, or invulnerable to the same kind of 'presentism' enacted by identity categories;[52] it too must be constantly challenged and criticized, if it is to remain effective at all. Indeed, in the past 10–15 years, queer has gained a legitimacy and institutional security which has contributed to its consolidation as a blanket-term for non-normative genders and sexualities, which is markedly different from its usage in the early 1990s. As Butler notes:

> If the term 'queer' is to be a site of collective contestation, the point of departure for a set of historical reflections and futural imaginings, it will have to remain that which is, in the present, never fully owned, but always only redeployed, twisted, queered from a prior usage and in the direction of urgent and expanding political purposes.[53]

The latent potentiality of queer, then, is that it acknowledges this very impossibility of completing the subject and the insufficiency of categorization in general, while also devising a way of challenging them. And in this sense, queer is best understood not as a new category of identity but as the assertion of a non-identity, and as a verb rather than a noun. Queer, as an activity and mode

---

[49] Blanchot, *Unavowable*, 56.
[50] David Halperin, *Saint Foucault: Towards a Gay Hagiography*, (Oxford, Oxford University Press 1995), 62. His emphasis.
[51] Nancy Fraser, 'The French Derrideans: Politicizing Deconstruction or Deconstructing the Political?' *New German Critique* 33 (1984), 127–54.
[52] Butler, *Gender Trouble*, 19.   [53] Butler, *Gender Trouble*, 19.

of communication, allows us in a sense to reach 'ecstasy' or that ecstatic beyond singular being which is a constitutive sharing, which for Bataille is a 'contestation of knowledge,' and could be seen as a resistance to discursive closure affected by universalized identity categories.[54] Queer affirmatively engages the excess of the world, using it to contest heteronormative society.

THANKS ARE OWED to Dan Matthews and Paisley Currah for providing comments on earlier drafts. Any oversights and shortcomings are my own.

---

[54] Georges Bataille, *Inner Experience* (Albany: State University of New York Press, 1988), 12.

— 6 —

Labour and Migration in the 'Suspended Step'

Anastasia Tataryn

Jean-Luc Nancy's notions of *sense* and the *sense of the world* offer a fundamentally different approach to immigration and employment/labour issues in the United Kingdom (UK). Commonly, in political discussions and media, workers categorized as 'migrant' bear the brunt of employment uncertainties sparked by labour market shifts in the UK.[1] One does not have to be well versed in British politics or immigration policies to recognise that claims, most notably by the United Kingdom Independence Party (UKIP), of foreign migrants imposing on the British labour market and impeding opportunities for British workers to hold decent jobs misdiagnose the forces at play in the British labour market.[2] Diagnosing, however, is not a simple task. Authors and legal

---

[1] Commonly, immigration and labour issues are discussed as a problem of migrant, meaning non-British, workers encroaching on the British domestic labour market. In the extreme, a migrant labour force is blamed for causing downward pressure on wages, for heightening precarious employment situations, and taking 'British' jobs from a national, citizen, labour force.

[2] The 'UKIP Local Manifesto 2014' states on the opening page, 'Open-door immigration is crippling local services in the UK' www.ukip.org. The perception of antagonism between migrants and citizens in the labour market has become normalized in many discussions of immigration control and (un)employment. For instance, Gordon Brown's infamous claim of 'British Jobs for British Workers' from 2007 has evolved into more sinister political platforms such as the 'go home' vans of the Home Office in 2013: Alan Travis, '"Go home" vans resulted in 11 people leaving Britain, says report' *The Guardian*, 31 October 2013.

academics express the difficulty of distilling the multiple interests surrounding labour, migration, and law, not only in the UK but internationally.³ The prevalence of exploitative labour situations and increasingly precarious forms of employment, particularly in low-waged sectors, demand attention, especially when workers continue to be subjugated in spite of human rights legislation and protective employment/labour laws.⁴ I draw on Jean-Luc Nancy's work on *sense,* thought through *exscription* and a *bodily ontology,* to respond to an ethical and philosophical demand to understand how and why particular categories guide political, juridical and economic discussions.⁵

My discussion here provides an outline of a larger project. I begin with an introduction to the exigency of labour migration and precarious work in the United Kingdom. I then highlight Nancy's thinking of exscription as it relates to the situation of persons identified as migrant labourers. This leads me to consider how Nancy's notion of *sense*—the *sense of the world* and our material bodily

---

³ International, European, and national interests that are economic as well as about protecting identity against foreigners intersect in issues of migration and labour. This causes conflicting priorities of protecting workers versus open borders and free movement of labour to clash. Many observers, academics, and policy analysts may feel at an impasse to ascertain how to discuss or move forward in matters of immigration and labour. Contradictory and countervailing interests converge and diverge and make it difficult to speak precisely of what is going on and why. See Chantal Thomas, 'Convergences and Divergences in International Legal Norms on Migrant Labour,' Comparative Labour Law and Policy Journal 32 (2011), 405–44. Kerry Rittich refers to the priorities of international labour standards as being guided by 'countervailing agendas': protection through core labour rights and promoting labour market flexibility for the benefit of financial institutions. These two priorities mean that, 'distributive justice for workers remains a pressing and elusive goal.' Kerry Rittich, 'Core Labour Rights and Labour Market Flexibility: Two Paths Entwined?' in *Labor Law Beyond Borders: ADR and the Internationalization of Labor Dispute Resolution,* ed. International Bureau of The Permanent Court of Arbitration (The Hague: Kluwer Law International, 2003), 157. Numerous UK statutes have been designed to remedy situations of vulnerability. For instance, United Kingdom: Asylum and Immigration (Treatment of Claimants, etc.) Act 2004; Coroners and Justice Act 2009, section 71; Gangmasters Licensing Act 2004; as well as more broadly the National Minimum Wage Act 1998, Employment Rights Act 1996 and Equalities Act 2010.

⁴ Much of what is experienced by 'migrant' workers is not captured within immigration and employment legislation. Furthermore the persistence of exploitative work environments reveals a gap between legal regulation (labour and immigration law) and employment practices—employment practices that, significantly, respond to labour market demand and supply and economic competitiveness.

⁵ Ian James, *Fragmentary Demand: An Introduction to the Philosophy of Jean-Luc Nancy* (Stanford: Stanford University Press, 2006), 150.

presence and participation—opens onto a dynamic ontological questioning where the situation of migrant and labour exposes much larger, fundamental shifts in concepts of being, nation state, and citizenship.[6]

The International Labour Organisation (ILO) estimates that, in 2014, there are approximately 232 million migrant workers worldwide.[7] Of these migrant workers, the International Organisation of Migration (IOM) estimates that 10 to 15 percent of are in irregular situations.[8] However, statistics determining this population are based on estimates. Definitions of who is counted as 'migrant worker' or 'irregular migrant worker' are often contested.[9] Identifying a migrant labour demographic is difficult, especially where these workers are neither clearly *illegal* nor recognized as asylum seekers or refugees.[10] What guides the search for identifying this population, however, is that increasingly there is a labour market demand for labourers who work in unregulated and exploitable labour situations. Labourers who are most often found in these situations are considered to be migrants, however precarious and vulnerable workers are not limited to those with foreign (non-national) status. The definition of precarious and

---

[6] When it comes to *sense*, there are two relevant aspects derived from Nancy's work that I maintain within focus of this discussion: first of all, that sense is a 'twilight border between absolute value (mythical discourse) and relative value (nihilist discourse),' a 'suspended step' between atomistic individuality and group identity. And secondly, that Being is functional, sense is concrete, and we know that there is 'something, and that alone makes sense.' Jean-Luc Nancy, *Sense of the World*, 2nd ed. (Minnesota: University of Minnesota Press, 2008), 7.

[7] International Labour Organisation, 'Labour Migration: Facts and figures' Fact Sheet, 26 March 2014. Accessed 24 November 2014, http://www.ilo.org/global/about-the-ilo/media-centre/issue-briefs/WCMS_239651/lang--en/index.htm.

[8] International Organisation for Migration (IOM) 'World Migration Report 2010. The future of migration: building capacities for change,' IOM, 2010, p. 29, Accessed 24 November 2014, http://publications.iom.int/bookstore/free/WMR_2010_ENGLISH.pdf.

[9] This is based on the difficulty to determine precisely who is considered a migrant and a lack of consistent definitions. For example, is a 'migrant' foreign-born or a foreign-national or person with a temporary work permit? See Bridget Anderson and Martin Ruhs, eds., *A Need for Migrant Labour? An introduction to the analysis of staff shortages, immigration and public policy* (Oxford: Oxford University Press, 2010); Scott Blinder, 'Briefing: UK Public Opinion Towards Immigration: Overall Attitudes and Level of Concern,' *Migration Observatory* (Oxford: University of Oxford, 2012).

[10] Provisions for asylum seekers (no work permit), or undocumented migrants who may be subjected to deportation or detention. See Nicholas De Genova and Nathalie Peutz, *The Deportation Regime: Sovereignty, Space, and the Freedom of Movement* (Durham, London: Duke University Press, 2010).

vulnerable workers concurrently implies, but is not exclusive to, persons working in low-waged, low-skilled labour sectors. In these sectors, for instance the service industry (fast-food workers) or agricultural food processing (packaging), the firms governing these labour sectors demand workers who live and work in conditions *as if* they were temporary migrant workers. The actual legal immigration status of persons in these jobs need not necessarily be precarious.[11] However, the employment insecurity of these workers, as a consequence of labour market demand, makes them economically precarious and socially devalued.

Immigration and labour, or 'migrant labour,' is a nexus of intersecting political, juridical, economic and cultural interests. These interests, when laid out and questioned, expose predetermined categories of recognition, which provide meaning and an order around which persons come together in a society, community, nation-state, and economic system. Categories of 'citizen,' 'migrant,' 'employee,' and 'foreign worker' allocate belonging ostensibly in the nation state. In practice, these categories ascribe recognition according to conditions of desirability that *make sense* of our sociality according to historically specific (ideological) paradigms of thought.

For instance, citizenship eludes strict definition.[12] Bridget Anderson contends that immigration and employment are riddled with notions of who is a 'Good Citizen' (worthy) versus a 'Failed Citizen' (undeserving).[13] The behaviour of Failed Citizens is juxtaposed with an elusive 'community of value,' maintained by those in positions of political and economic power or dominance. The failure of persons to keep up with the community of value is used

---

[11] EU workers, for instance are entitled to the freedom of labour and work equal to citizens. The EU freedom of movement further complicates the distinction between 'migrant' and 'citizen.' Membership in the EU allows citizens of European Union (EU) member states the freedom to work in the UK with rights equal to British citizens (According to the European Parliament and Council Directive 2004/38/EC article 20). Nevertheless, a 'migrant' status, when an individuals' identity is signified as foreign or non-citizens, assumes that these individuals are precariously present in Britain. This status can be the result of racialization and ethnicisation, and not a legal status. Maria Hudson, Gina Netto et al., *In-work poverty, ethnicity and workplace cultures* (London: Joseph Rowntree Foundation, 2013).

[12] Anne McNevin, *Contesting Citizenship: Irregular Migrants and New Frontiers of the Political* (Columbia: Columbia University Press, 2011).

[13] Bridget Anderson, *Us & Them: The Dangerous Politics of Immigration Control* (Oxford: Oxford University Press, 2013), 2–5.

as justification for their working in precarious, low-waged, jobs where they are excluded from the ambit of protective labour law.

The Good Citizen and Failed Citizen are not categories based on formal legal statuses. Rather, the idea of citizenship is based on a notion of who participates in a shared community of value, the shared set of social practices and norms that are seen to exemplify citizenship.[14] For example, discourses used by the UK government that speak of 'hard working British citizens' contrast with ideas of 'lazy benefit scroungers' or persons dependent on state support who are a burden to the country. Often, the latter are identified as part of a racial or ethnic group that is not British. Indeed, Failed Citizens are those who have not managed to keep up within the shared set of values set by the dominant Anglo (white, male) elite. Historically, these sub-citizens have included vagrants, women,[15] colonial subjects, slaves or indentured servants,[16] disabled persons,[17] prison inmates[18] and children.[19] Thus, although citizenship remains the measure of formal recognition in the nation state, legally possessing citizenship status does not ensure equal recognition of rights in the nation state.[20] For workers in precarious employment, where they are vulnerable to be exploited for their labour, holding citizenship status or a work permit as a migrant foreign worker can make little difference. Notwithstanding the extreme situations of individuals and families without legal immigration status or work permits, persons who are treated as if they were migrants and undocumented are part of an increasingly widespread labour market demand for a cheap, flexible, temporary, and exploitable workforce.[21]

---

[14] Anderson, *Us & Them*, 5.

[15] Joanne Conaghan and Kerry Rittich, eds., *Labour Law, Work, and Family: Critical and Comparative Perspectives* (Oxford: Oxford University Press, 2005), 8.

[16] Adelle Blackett, 'Emancipation in the Idea of Labour Law,' in Guy Davidov and Brian Langille, eds., *The Idea of Labour Law* (Oxford: Oxford University Press, 2011), 420–1.

[17] Jihan Abbas, 'A Legacy of Exploitation: Intellectual disability, unpaid labour and disability services' *New Politics* 14/1 (2012), 53.

[18] Noah Zatz, 'Working at the Boundaries of Markets: Prison Labor and the Economic Dimension of Employment Relationships' *Vanderbuilt Law Review* 61 (2008) 857–958.

[19] Geraldine Van Beuren, *The International Law on the Rights of the Child* (The Hague: Martinus Nijhoff Publishers, 1998), 263.

[20] Anderson, *Us & Them*, 4. However, I do not deny that persons without legal documentation or without permission to live and work in the UK are most vulnerable to labour exploitation.

[21] Persons treated 'as if migrant workers' is my phrase to refer to the situations of

Processes of neoliberalization within the ostensibly global market economic system capitalize on the assumption that precarious workers in low-waged, low-skilled labour are migrants.[22] The *Global Cities at Work* project in London refers to the emphasis, and benefit derived from this assumption, through their investigation of the 'migrant division of labour.'[23] The term 'migrant' connotes non-citizenship and non-permanence. This can serve to justify maintaining workers in precarious labour situations. Precarious labour situations mean that based on their employment contract these individuals do not have access to full employment status via a standard employment relationship. Subsequently, legal protections established in UK employment law can be avoided, even for those who may hold citizenship status.[24] Meanwhile the labour market dependence on workers maintained in precarious and exploitable labour situations (non-British nationals and citizens alike) is obscured. As individuals come up against regimes of immigration control and employment regulation, the experience (actual, physical and material coming together) of labour and migration are removed from recognized categories of employment and immigration.

The migration of workers from outside the UK is depicted in popular media and political debates as a threat to the employment opportunities of citizen workers. However, sustained economic analyses of the British labour market indicate that migrant labour (and immigration) does not have a direct displacement effect on a British-citizen workforce.[25] Both foreign nationals and citizens are

---

in-work poverty, exacerbated through current trends of zero-hour contracts, agency sub-contracting, lack of investment in training opportunities or career progression in low-paid labour work. Informal recruitment practices, lack of integration of equality and diversity policies into workplace contexts, lack of resources to invest in development, as well as workplace cultures that under-report bad practices, including a reluctance or inability to voice opposition in the workplace, contribute to 'low-wage traps' Marie Hudson, Gina Netto, et al. *In-Work Poverty, Ethnicity and Workplace Cultures* (London: Joseph Rowantree Foundation, 2013).

[22] Jaime Peck, Nik Theodore and Neil Brennar, 'Neoliberalism Resurgent? Market Rule after the Great Recession' *The South Atlantic Quarterly* 111/2 (2012), 268.

[23] Jane Wills et al., *Global cities at work: New migrant divisions of labour* (London, New York: Pluto Press, 2010).

[24] Bridget Anderson and Martin Ruhs, 'Reliance on Migrant Labour: inevitability or policy choice?' *Journal of Poverty and Social Justice* 20 (2012), 23–30.

[25] Christian Dustmann, Tommaso Frattini, and Ian Preston, 'The Effect of Immigration along the Distribution of Wages,' *Review of Economic Studies* 80 (2013), 145–173; Christian Dustman and Ian Preston, 'Estimating the Effect of Immigration on Wages,' *Journal of the European Economic Association* 10 (2011), 216–23.

affected by labour market shifts. Global firms rely heavily on subcontracted and agency labour, across jurisdictional and territorial boundaries, while immigration and labour/employment law remain rooted in traditional frameworks of the territorially-bounded nation-state and standard contractual employment relationship. Where labour markets (demand and supply of work) quickly respond to ostensibly global labour markets, legal protections and regulations are slow to follow. Consequently, individuals who work in low-waged sectors whose employment relationship is outside the legally recognized standard contractual employment relationship and who are neither clearly foreign, temporary migrants, nor recognized as British citizens slip into gaps of the law.[26] Firms seeking cheap labour to maintain their economic competitiveness in the global market may prefer workers in these gaps or legal grey areas. Employing these temporary, shadowed workers allows employers to avoid existing regulations and protections.

It may seem that these legal gaps are what Nancy has described as the *exscription,* or what is *excribed*. For example, these workers ('migrant' 'vulnerable' 'precarious' 'shadowed') are written out of the text of labour laws, they are living and working beyond the standard, normal legal labour regime. Yet exscription is not in opposition and neither is it 'uninscribable.' Rather, exscription reveals the end that is the limit from which *sense* is the unravelling and re-ravelling of inscription and exscription.[27] Persons relegated to legal grey areas are not captured by the term "exscription". Rather, persons who are in the shadow of the labour market still participate and play a vital role in the labour market. The workers who provide cheap, exploitable labour are in demand and thus condition the labour market. In fact, they are *inscribed* as irregular migrant labour.

Exscription is not a word or an event that can be named, according to Nancy, without 'being mangled by one's own barbarism.'[28] To

---

[26] See Leah Vosko, *Managing the Margins: Gender, Citizenship and the International Regulation of Precarious Employment* (Oxford: Oxford University Press, 2010), 1. By precarious situation I mean work that is insecure, low-waged, characterised by a lack of opportunities for career development and training. See Maria Hudson, Gina Netto, et al., *In-Work Poverty, Ethnicity and Workplace Cultures* (London: Joseph Rowntree Foundation, 2013).

[27] Nancy, *Sense of the World*, 11.

[28] Jean-Luc Nancy and Katherine Lydon, 'Exscription,' *Yale French Studies* 78 (1990), 64.

write and to inscribe what *exscription* is, is to continue *exscribing*: 'writing, reading, I exscribe the thing itself, "existence," the "real"— which is only exscribed and whose *being* alone is what's at stake in inscription.'[29] Exscription challenges us to think about what is written out of the text of both the legal protection and labour practices. The factors that are 'written out of the text' are not external influences, but are excess from within.[30] In other words, exscription is an instance of community's resistance, a 'moment—when the in of the 'in-common' erupts, resists, and disrupts the relations of need and force—annuls collective and communal hypostases.'[31]

Exscription helps to conceive of how labour has, on the one hand, been inscribed into the market and the nation state, while on the other hand, the 'ethic of the market' denies what it exscribes away from itself.[32] The ethic of the market, embedded in the nation state, projects a narrative of inclusion and tolerance while establishing an exclusionary agenda.[33] In neoliberalism, market exchange is seen as

> 'an ethic in itself, capable of acting as a guide to all human action, and substituting for all previously held ethical beliefs,' it [i.e. Neoliberalism] holds that the social good [which is commonly recognized as coming through the nation-state] will be maximized by maximizing the reach and frequency of market transactions.[34]

The ethic of the market makes it seem necessary, but also inevitable, for the nation state to converge with the market. This is opposed to the practice of the market, which constantly exceeds and over-rides the bounds of the nation state. The market responds to the more fluid community of value, while espousing the nation state and its ideals of formal citizenship. Thus the community of value and labour market converge in what Jaime Peck, Nick Brennar and Neil Theodore term neoliberalization: an ongoing process that is 'a

---

[29] Nancy, 'Exscription,' 64.

[30] Jacques Derrida, *On Touching—Jean-Luc Nancy* (Stanford: Stanford University Press, 2004), 299.

[31] Jean-Luc Nancy, *The Inoperative Community* (Minnesota: University of Minnesota, 1991), xl.

[32] Jacques Derrida, *On Touching—Jean-Luc Nancy*, 299.

[33] For more on this, see Hans Lindahl, 'In Between: Immigration, Distributive Justice, and Political Dialogue' *Contemporary Political Theory* 8/4 (2009), 415–34.

[34] David Harvey, *A Brief History of Neoliberalism* (Oxford: Oxford University Press, 2005), 3.

crisis induced, crisis inducing form of market-disciplinary regulatory restructuring.'[35] Labour situations that demand cheap, flexible, exploitable workers are a consequence of neoliberalization and a purportedly global market economy, not an influx of non-citizen, migrant workers.

The inscription that happens through categories that distinguish an inside (citizen) versus an outside (migrant) *signifies* the movement of workers within the labour market in which they participate. The labour market has developed as the lens of intelligibility that allows labour and labourers to be recognized within the dominant legal and economic system. However, the market itself is a historically specific construct. It has come to be seen as if it were the only way to understand labour and employment through categories that are believed to signify the totality of who is participating inside or outside the nation state, and the 'globalized' economic market. This signification, as Meurs and Devisch's contribution to this collection discusses, is different from *sense*.[36] *Sense* challenges categories that through legislation and legal practice are *made* to *make Sense*.[37] Rather than refer to a closed relation, *sense* is the presentation, the happening or co-appearance, of being in the world. Sense pre-exists signification and is *the* challenge to closed representations because it is the very being, action, of our world.

It is important to distinguish *sense* from *signification* or categories, labels, which are *made* to *make* sense such that they go unquestioned. For instance, in labour and migration, the sense of people coming together as producing, working beings has been inscribed into the market economic system by categories of work and statuses. Action and production is interpreted and recognized based on the market, where one is either participating as a worker, in a contractual relationship (contract of service or for services), or alternatively is engaged in lesser-valued 'non-market' labour.[38] The inscription of labour via the paradigm of the market means

---

[35] Jaime Peck, Nik Theodore, and Neil Brennar, 'Neoliberalism Resurgent? Market Rule after the Great Recession' *The South Atlantic Quarterly* 111/2 (Spring 2012), 268.

[36] *Signification*, meaning to bring into a fixed, closed relationship; see p. 47–8.

[37] I refer to Nancy's use of the term 'sense' in italics—this is the sense that is the happening of exscription/inscription, the touching on what is beyond but simultaneously part of the concretion of the world. Sense, with a capital 'S', is what is made-to-make-sense and be comprehensible within existing dominant paradigms.

[38] For the distinction between a contract of service and for services, see *Market Investigations Ltd v Minister for Social Security* [1969] 2 QB 173.

that individuals are recognized as legal subjects and participants based on their economic productivity and value. Consequently, from economic productivity and worth, individuals are granted status as members of the national community of value—they are Good Citizens.

Nancy's *sense* lays bare what we have as the world as our corporeal experience, at the very occurrence of thought and thinking. Here, sense is 'the concept of the concept.'[39] Following from such a process, thinking of the sense happening in labour and migration involves questioning which bodies are working, which bodies are employed, where and under what circumstances. And which bodies benefit.

The experiences in labour practices invariably push beyond recognized, legally formalized, categories. Practically speaking, this disconnect between the experiences exscribed and the categories that formally define membership in a nation state, when experienced in a city such as London, UK—where masses of people come together in spaces, as visitors, residents, natives, with varying degrees of legal subjectivity—renders the formal categories incoherent and to a large extent, elusive to experience. The precariousness and insecurity that has been identified in employment and blamed on foreign migrants has become a technique of economic power in global economic markets.

The *sense* 'on the ground' and the Sense that is made are together what *make* the *sense of the world*. If we are to answer to the imperative of the situations where labourers are rendered vulnerable and precarious, with the realisation that the operative categories do not address what is actually happening with employment practices, then our approach must strive to reconceptualize labour and law through this different lens. The challenge is to grapple with the need for a frame and the knowledge that the frame will always be questioned and confronted. Scholars thinking about the intersections of labour, migration, and precarious work have proposed international, rights-based, constitutional or cosmopolitan-based alternatives for labour and law.[40] Notwithstanding the importance

---

[39] Jean-Luc Nancy, *A Finite Thinking* (Stanford: Stanford University Press, 2003), 5. A reflection that suggests 'applying' or 'using' Nancy's work runs the risk of betraying the challenge at the core of his thought. Nancy challenges the operative, programme-oriented paradigm that many responses to social and political issues entail.

[40] Catherine Dauvergne, *Making People Illegal* (Cambridge: Cambridge University

of these approaches, Nancy shift attention away from these alternatives to instead challenge us to question the foundation that creates and constitutes the imperative for categories and ultimately the boundaries and limits of law.

A labour force that is inscribed as existing outside the ambit of regular legal frameworks, as 'migrant,' presents a challenge to fundamental frameworks of law, as well as to notions of social participation and citizenship. As academics and writers, we grapple with the resistance and challenge presented by Nancy within our own work as much as we do within the social, political and economic exigencies we research. Adhering to Nancy's challenge would entail resisting the compulsion to reinforce standard paradigms of thought, avoiding the

> wish to dress the wound with the usual tatters of worn-out finery: god or money, petrol or muscle, information or incantation [new words, new concepts] which always ends up signifying one form or another of all-powerfulness and all-presence.[41]

Indeed, thinking of the precariousness in between or beyond language—as present and as *existing*—is not satisfying work. Neither does it give us a pragmatic answer. Yet for labour, migration, and law, when we grapple with the vast temporality and space of work and action, activity and identity, bringing *sense* into the frame, as attention to *exscription*, can bring awareness of the precariousness that *is*. That is, the coming together of bodies in common that is uncertain, but certain to happen. The question remains, what changes to our thinking are possible when the making Sense and *sense* that is *exscribed* inform a continuing resistance to seemingly necessary, inevitable categories of neoliberalization and order (labour markets and citizenship). This resistance is one that *is*, and is not from the outside, but from within the very happening, experience, and existence of the world.

Press, 2008); Brian Langille, 'Labour Law's Theory of Justice,' in *The Idea of Labour Law*, ed. Guy Davidov and Brian Langille (Oxford: Oxford University Press, 2011), 101–119.

[41] Jean-Luc Nancy, 'The Confronted Community,' trans. Amanda Macdonald, *Post-Colonial Studies* 6/1 (2003), 24.

— 7 —

Survival's Witness: Poetry, Sociality, Community

Patrick Hanafin

No law rules poetry.[1]

If testimony... became proof, information, certainty, or archive, it would lose its function as testimony. In order to remain testimony, it must ... allow itself to be haunted. It must allow itself to be parasitized by precisely what it excludes from its inner depths, the possibility, at least of literature.[2]

There is no work of art that does not call on a people who does not exist.[3]

The norms against which we struggle are social norms and they govern us as social creatures, we make ourselves with others and only on the condition that there are forms of collectivity that are struggling against the norms in similar convergent ways.[4]

Writing [is] a way of coming back to life ... of being in this life.[5]

---

[1] Gerald L. Bruns, *Maurice Blanchot: The Refusal of Philosophy* (Baltimore: Johns Hopkins University Press, 1997), 84.

[2] Jacques Derrida, Demeure: Fiction and Testimony (Stanford: Stanford Universirty Press), 29–30.

[3] Gilles Deleuze, *Two Regimes of Madness* (New York: Semiotexte, 2006), 324.

[4] Judith Butler and Athena Athanasiou, *Dispossession: The Performative in the Political* (Cambridge: Polity, 2013), 67.

[5] David Grossman, Interview, *Front Row*, BBC Radio 4, 21 February 2014.

In her analysis of survivability, vulnerability, and affect in her book *Frames of War*, Judith Butler provides us with an example of what I would term a poetic sociality.[6] In the first chapter of the book, Butler analyzes the anthology of poems written by detainees in Guantanamo Bay prison camp. The collection, *Poems from Guantanamo: The Detainees Speak*, comprises twenty-two poems which survived the censor's pen.[7] The event of the writing of these poems testifies to a living on of the bare lives contained within the confines of the camp. Such a writing disrupts the normative order of the camp where the inquisitor rules and attempts to extract words from the mouths of the detainees. In the exceptional state of the internment camp, what is important is the way in which all aspects of life are governed and behaviour is modified so that internees become mollified and compliant citizens. This dictation of what one does in the camp is intended to make all acts predictable. When words come forth in unexpected places, such as in a poem, and without being forced, then what occurs is, in Judith Butler's terms, a rupturing of the frame of the acceptable and the conditioned. The poems become 'part of the very process through which new contexts are delimited and formed.'[8]

This undoing of the ordered and conditioned world of the camp is highlighted by the reaction of the censors in the US Department of Defense to the very writing of these poems. Indeed, as the editor of *Poems from Guantanamo*, the lawyer Marc Falkoff, observes in his introduction to the collection, the fear provoked by such writing led the authorities to respond in a violent and censorious manner:

> Many of the detainees' poems were destroyed or confiscated before they could be shared with the authors' lawyers. ... [T]he Pentagon refuses to allow most of the detainees' poems to be made public, arguing that poetry 'presents a special risk' to national security because of its 'content and format.' The fear appears to be that the detainees will try to smuggle coded messages out of the prison camp. Hundreds of poems therefore remain suppressed by the military and will likely never be seen by the public. ... [M]ost of the poems that have been cleared are in English translation only, because the Pentagon believes that their original Arabic or Pashto versions

---

[6] Judith Butler, *Frames of War: When Is Life Grieveable?* (London: Verso, 2009).
[7] Marc Falkoff, ed., *Poems from Guantanamo: The Detainees Speak* (Iowa City: University of Iowa Press, 2007).
[8] Butler, *Frames of War*, 9.

represent an enhanced security risk.[9]

It is as if these words, neither provoked by torture nor elicited by force, are somehow suspect and carriers of secret and threatening messages. If the state fears poetry then we have to be concerned about the kind of polity in which we exist and the kind of community which it valorizes. The kind of community that such a state endorses is one in which citizens are mere purveyors of information, subjects formed and constructed by the state in order to secure its continued existence. Such subjects are not counted as individual living beings but merely as objects to be governed or made to act. They are abstract whats rather than individual whos. The unique existent is the contrary of the *what* of universal humanism. It is the *who* of the unique self, possessed of her own speech, her own narrative, which she relates to another unique existent. This unique individual who refuses to be styled by power is a threat to the biopolitical order. This unique existent cannot be managed, made to speak in the language of the state, or be manipulated for biopolitical purposes. In a biopolitical model where the regularity of the what is favoured over the unpredictable who, the unexpected is both feared and the object of suspicion. If words are seen as threats to the security of the state, then the paradigm of state sovereignty under which we live is one in which the citizen is viewed as an object of governance whom the state makes speak. The reaction of the American state to words written out of context, outside or beyond the ordered frame of things, points to an anxiety on the part of the state towards those who, for it, represent disorder or insubordination.

In the camp what is important is that all aspects of life are governed by rules. This dictation of what one does in the camp makes all acts predictable and foreseeable and thereby subject to biopolitical control. There is no unpredictability. The disorderly word, the word not sought or extracted by the inquisitor provokes a shocked reaction on behalf of the state. In this regard, the manner in which the camp is ordered provides an example in microcosm of the biopolitical state. As subjects of power, we are expected to behave in certain approved ways. Unexpected or insubordinate ways of being are not encouraged. These poems testify to a

---

[9] Marc Falkoff, 'Notes on Guantanamo,' in Falkoff, *Poems*, 4–5, 5.

short-circuiting of the order of the camp. In another sense they expose the fiction of all power and law in its attempt to create order and to control citizens' behaviour. The reaction of the state to the disorderly sociality of the Guantanamo Bay inmates mirrors the way in which the state tries to control citizens in the wider polity. The objective of communication for the state is as a means of ordering and shaping the citizen rather than as a means of being with others in community. The act of the prisoners points to a fundamental disjunction between seeing community as a means of nation-building and seeing community as a mode of being with others; between, in other words, an operative and an inoperative community.

The inoperativity of the poets' performance brings forth a body and a voice from within the boundaries of imposed subjectivity. This being, in literature, of those excluded from the polity speaks to what Jean-Luc Nancy has called an 'inoperative community' which challenges the imposition of identity and subjectivity and calls for an impersonal being-in-common of singular beings.[10] In this regard, the poems express another thinking of subjectivity which escapes the ordering and categorizing function of the always operative state. This inoperative act of poetry allows the individual voices of unique existents to appear. Such unique beings are the contrary of the *what* of the ordered subject of law. The *who* of the unique self relates to other unique existents through their words and in so doing undoes the imposed models of community and citizenship, creating instead a more disorganized assemblage of unique individuals which exists beyond the *polis* as organized political community.

Poetry Against the Law

The communication of the inmates' stubborn being-there in poetry has, to paraphrase Jean-Luc Nancy, 'the precise structure of and nature of a being in writing, of a "literary" being: it resides only in the communication—which does not commune—of its advance and retreat.'[11] This has implications for the way in which we think community, sovereignty, and rights in liberal polities, by undoing the imposed separation in liberal discourse of the political subject

---

[10] Jean-Luc Nancy, *The Inoperative Community* (Minneapolis: University of Minnesota Press, 1991).

[11] Nancy, *Inoperative Community*, 78.

from its body and its voice. It also provides us with a means to think a praxis of inoperativity as resistance.[12] The fact that such singularities choose to expose themselves through the medium of poetry is important. Poetry contains a secret, not the secret that the state would like to extract by force, but a secret beyond any informational utility in the state's ongoing war on terror and in its attempt to shape and form the citizen subject. As J. M. Coetzee has put it:

> The masters of information have forgotten about poetry, where words may have a meaning quite different from what the lexicon says, where the metaphoric spark is always one jump ahead of the decoding function, where another, unforeseen reading is always possible.[13]

Indeed the operative community of neoliberal modernity is one in which words are contained and policed. The ordered state forces words from citizens' mouths, not one's own willed words, but words which represent the Truth for the inquisitor, the definitive word, the measurable word, the word that counts as information. The metaphoric spark of poetry goes beyond the expected response to the imposed relation of citizen and state and the available response of citizens to biopower.

These poems counter the useful speech extracted under torture and reverse the ordered dyadic relationship of inquisitor and victim. As Maurice Blanchot has put it:

> The Powerful One is the master of the possible, but he is not master of this relation that does not derive from mastery and that power cannot measure: the relation without relation wherein the 'other' is revealed as 'autrui.' … Hence the furious movement of the inquisitor who wants by force to obtain a scrap of language in order to bring all speech down to the level of force. To make speak, and through torture, is to attempt to master infinite distance by reducing expression to this language of power through which the one who speaks would once again lay himself open to force's hold; and the one who is being tortured refuses to speak in order not to enter through the extorted words into the game of opposing violence, but also, at the same time, in order to preserve the true speech that he very well

---

[12] See further, Arne De Boever, 'Overhearing Bartleby: Agamben, Melville, and Inoperative Power,' *Parrhesia* 1 (2006), 144.

[13] J. M. Coetzee, *Diary of a Bad Year* (London: Vintage, 2008), 23.

knows is at this instant merged with his silent presence—which is the very presence of *autrui* in himself.[14]

In the case of the Guantanamo poets we witness the reversal of the relationship of inquisitor and victim. The poets' words resist and escape capture and ordering, and, in so doing, testify to the writers' wanting 'to be present without letting [themselves] be defined, accounted for, explained.'[15] This creates an interruption or reversal in the normal relationship of prisoners and guards. Such a writing resists being incorporated into regimes of power and refuses to be categorized by the speech of law. The surprising word which issues from nowhere, authorized by no one has no end other than as an appeal, a testimony of just being there, of surviving. It refuses the unequal relationship of torturer and victim. What we witness here is a move from forced confession to a contestation of the forced extraction of speech. What the poems do is, to borrow Judith Butler's term, to put 'life into truthful form.'[16]

This is writing as a means of refusing the imposed order of things. Indeed as Judith Butler has observed, the poems of these Guantanamo detainees

> are critical acts of resistance, insurgent interpretations, incendiary acts that somehow, incredibly, live through the violence they oppose, even if we do not yet know in what ways such lives will survive.[17]

The poem is then both appeal and testimony and allows us a different means of conceptualizing sociality, a sociality beyond yet within the law of the camp. For Butler:

> In these poems, the body is also what lives on, breathes, tries to carve its breath into stone; its breathing is precarious—it can be stopped by the force of another's torture. But if this precarious status can become the condition of suffering, it also serves the condition of responsiveness, of a formulation of affect, understood as a radical

---

[14] Maurice Blanchot, *The Infinite Conversation* (Minneapolis: The University of Minnesota Press, 1993), 132.

[15] De Boever, *Overhearing Bartleby*, 149.

[16] Stuart Murray and Judith Butler, 'Ethics at the Scene of Address: A Conversation with Judith Butler,' *Symposium: Review of the Canadian Journal for Continental Philosophy* 11 (2007), 415–45, 416.

[17] Butler, *Frames of War*, 62.

act of interpretation in the face of unwilled subjugation.[18]

Poetry, in this sense, creates a space wherein lies the imperfection of permanently provisional and precarious lives. As such, it threatens all attempts by the polity to create achieved and complete subjects. The poems bear testimony to stubborn life, to the unruly reality of material selves. As Judith Butler notes of the writers of these poems:

> The lives of those at Guantanamo do not count as the kind of 'human lives' protected by human rights discourse. The poems themselves offer a different kind of moral responsiveness, a kind of interpretation that may, under certain conditions, contest and explode the dominant schisms running through the national and military ideology. The poems both constitute and convey a moral responsiveness to a military rationale that has restricted moral responsiveness to violence in incoherent and unjust ways.[19]

For Butler the writing of these poems can be seen as an effort 'to re-establish a social connection to the world, even where there is no concrete reason to think that any such connection is possible.'[20] As such this writing allows us to trace an 'originary sociality' beyond the bounds of the necropolitical state formation.[21] This testament to an originary sociality is provided by a stubborn living on of those written out of the liberal narrative of subjecthood and rights protection. Such a survival bears testimony to another way of being together, a communication of an inoperative community performed by the exposure to another, as opposed to the acceptable speech of the atomistic in a rigidly delineated polity.

This inoperative community of communication and exposure does not attempt to found a new community nor to inscribe a territory. It is rather what Étienne Balibar calls an 'anti-territory within the territory,'[22] an inoperative sociality. These words which circulated on unexpected objects, foam cups on which the words were engraved with small rocks or pebbles, testify to the continued

---

[18] Butler, *Frames of War*, 61. [19] Butler, *Frames of War*, 62.
[20] Butler, *Frames of War*, 59–60.
[21] Re 'originary sociality,' see Nancy, *Inoperative Community*, 28.
[22] Étienne Balibar, 'A Thought Of/From The Outside: Foucault's Uses of Blanchot' (lecture delivered at the Centre for Research in Modern European Philosophy and the London Graduate School, Kingston University, London, 21 February 2013).

living of the writers despite the attempt by power to silence them. The performance of the writing of these poems signifies a resistance to surrender to the role imposed on the detainee as source of information. In Judith Butler's formulation, such a mode of writing can be seen as both 'evidence and... appeal, in which each word is finally meant for another.'[23] For Butler, 'once the breath is made into words, the body is given over to another, in the form of an appeal.'[24] These words break free of the frame of the prison camp and circulate elsewhere. Such powerless words have an effect in the world, even if this is not an immediate transformation of the writers' lives. As Butler puts it:

> The movement of the ... text outside of confinement is a kind of 'breaking out,' so that even though ... the poetry can[not] free anyone from prison ... [the poems] nevertheless ... provide the conditions for breaking out of the quotidian acceptance of war and for a more generalized horror and outrage that will support and impel calls for justice and an end to violence.[25]

For Butler, the 'forming of words may be linked to survivability.'[26] This living on of the word beyond the circumstances of the camp is a call for a greater justice beyond the law which regulates and governs the camp. As such, these poems represent what Gerald Bruns has described as 'the unreconstructed voice of the singular and the irreducible, that which cannot be assimilated into a system or theory of constituted subjects, objects, and relations.'[27]

Words Beyond the Law

Law attempts to provide a frame to construct or put to work the polity. It creates the textual illusion of a community founded on a being in common. In this regard, law can be seen as a stabilizing instrument, a means of suspending in abstract ghostly form identifiable citizens who are simultaneously citizens with an identity. In other words, the text of law creates or provokes a symbolic unity

---

[23] Judith Butler, *Frames of War: When Is Life Grievable?* (London: Verso, 2009), 59.
[24] Butler, *Frames of War*, 61.   [25] Butler, *Frames of War*, 11.
[26] Judith Butler, 'Vulnerability/Survivability: The Affective Politics of War,' (lecture delivered at the Birkbeck Institute of Social Research, Birkbeck College, London, 27 February 2008).
[27] Bruns, *The Refusal of Philosophy*, xvi.

where none exists in order to secure the state in its territorial and textual space. However this grounded commonality of the state shares discursive space with a formless community, which constantly interrupts it, as the possibility of community beyond the juridico-political state formation. Such an inoperative community lives with the order of the law not distinct from it or as an alternative to it. The Guantanamo Bay poets' intervention provides a clear example of such an inoperative living-with legality. In other words the legal description and defining of citizens is not the last word on possible ways of being in society. Indeed to take it as the last word is a surrender to the ordering of citizens by biopower. For Judith Butler we are mistaken if 'we take the definitions of who we are, legally, to be adequate descriptions of what we are about.'[28] The Guantanamo Poets are an instantiation of another political community and expose the false binary between poetry and philosophy, order and disorder, thought and action, and speech and voice. The antinomy contained within the space of order can be seen in these poems very being-there. The existence of these poems constitutes an escape of words from a 'no-where,' an a-topia, words from nowhere authorized by no one. This poetry then is not the marking of an end, but rather an appeal addressed to another.

This ephemeral writing of dissent calls silently to a time beyond the present order. These poems in their varied ways are a testament to an injustice which the law of the camp and of the polity condones. More precisely these are what remain or survive of such testimony given the large scale censorship of the poems. These poems reveal a desire for an impossible justice, impossible precisely in the context of the legal machinery of the so-called war on terror. As far as the law is concerned the detainees are non-persons and can be dealt with impunity. As Giorgio Agamben has put it they: 'are subject ... only to raw power; they have no legal existence.'[29] Indeed the appeal to another for a justice beyond the law is evident in the poems. This is clear in the deathly appeal of Jumah al-Dossari's 'Death Poem':

---

[28] Judith Butler, *Precarious Life: The Powers of Mourning and Violence* (London: Verso, 2006), 25.

[29] Ulrich Raulff, 'Interview with Giorgio Agamben: Life, A Work of Art Without an Author: The State of Exception, the Administration of Disorder and Private Life,' *German Law Journal* 5 (2004), 610, http://www.germanlawjournal.com/article.php?id=437.

> Take my blood.
> Take my death shroud and
> The remnants of my body.
> Take photographs of my corpse at the grave, lonely.
> Send them to the world,
> To the judges and
> To the people of conscience,
> Send them to the principled men and the fair-minded.
> And let them bear the guilty burden, before the world,
> Of this innocent soul.
> Let them bear the burden, before their children and before history,
> Of this wasted, sinless soul,
> Of this soul which has suffered at the hands of the 'protectors of peace.'[30]

Such a spectral appeal is to another justice beyond the confines of the legality of the camp, of the state of exception, and of the thanatopolitical state formation.

This performance as well as testimony to suffering and violence is also a call to responsibility and justice, an ethical act. It is, to paraphrase Roberto Esposito, 'a demand, on the part of justice, "for ever greater justice."'[31] When such material singularities as the Guantanamo poets come together to act in common, we witness what Esposito envisages as a politics *of* life not a politics *over* life.[32] In other words, it is a politics which does not valorize an abstract, ideologically rigid notion of Life which restricts individual lives, but rather a politics of life which is driven by actions of individual living beings acting in relation with one another. It enacts an impersonal force which dissolves the enforced distinction between *bios* and *zoe*—between the homogeneous non-differentiated subject of power and the flesh of individual lives—and reveals instead singularity in difference. This overcoming of the separation between bare life and Life is a continuous task, a work in progress, a becoming, and a continual beginning, performed by an unavowable community of the not yet assimilated.[33] Such a performance of community

---

[30] Jumah al-Dossari, 'Death Poem,' in Falkoff, *Poems*, 32.

[31] Roberto Esposito, *Terza Persona: Politica della vita e filosofia dell'impersonale* (Torino: Einaudi, 2007), 132.

[32] Esposito, *Terza Persona*, 185.

[33] See further Miguel Vatter, 'Biopolitics: From Surplus Value to Surplus Life,' *Theory & Event* 12 (2009), DOI: 10.1353/tae.0.0062.

provides an opening to the future, not a monumentalization of the past. This inoperative poetic sociality opposes the model of subject identity formation in the modern state. It does not come in response to a demand or interrogation but rather emerges from the margins unsolicited, an instance of 'unexpected speech.'[34] This thinking with and against a law of ordering allows us to think writing not as a work in the sense of a completed object, a monument to memory, but an opening to the future. These words come not in response to a demand for truth. Instead they exemplify the impossibility of a subject forming narrative and the concomitant possibility of another mode of being together in relation with others. This negative affirmation of agency by those not deemed worthy of full legal personhood can be seen as an instance of the stubborn refusal of mere life to be categorized and ruled. It is a refusal to surrender to the role imposed on the detainee as objects containing information vital to the security of the state. The poets leave traces but are not traced and formed by the law. Their words perform what Michel Foucault has called: '[the] right to bear witness, to oppose truth to power.... That right to set a powerless truth against a truthless power.'[35]

Conclusion

In the inoperative community of poetic sociality of the Guantanamo Bay poets, the word is not some abstract order which law imposes on, or forces from one, but *is* politics. The act of speaking and writing becomes a political act which refuses subordination by the state. One speaks as a unique existent, as a *who* and, in so doing, disrupts the symbolic representation of the detainee as pure voice deprived of speech. This uniqueness cannot be captured by or conditioned by the fact of citizenship or legal subjectivity. Such unique selves, as Hannah Arendt observed, reveal themselves through both speech and action. For Arendt:

> In acting and speaking, men show who they are, reveal actively their unique personal identities and thus make their appearance in the human world, while their physical identities appear without any

---

[34] Maurice Blanchot, *Les Intellectuels en question* (Tours: Farrago, 2000), 36.
[35] Michel Foucault, 'Truth and Juridical Forms,' in *Michel Foucault: Essential Works 1954–84, Volume 3: Power*, ed. James D. Faubion (London: Penguin, 2002), 33.

activity of their own in the unique shape of the body and sound of the voice.[36]

Such an episode testifies that there will always remain a *physis* beyond the control of the *polis*. The Guantanamo Bay poets' acts of resistance are carried out in the most passive and harmless of ways, through writing. In so doing, they break the cycle of violence and counter-violence. These poems are not an attempt to appropriate through violence the power of speech. Instead these poems are, in the words of Jean-Luc Nancy, a: 'way of covering a territory of words, not in order to find something, or to plant a crop, or to build an edifice, but simply to measure it.'[37] For Nancy, what all poetry cannot accept and resists is

> that the 'form' in question can envelop or enclose itself and 'form itself' ... on the basis of its own denial. ... [T]his refusal itself is poetry, and even if 'poetry' remains or appears, at this particular moment, to be completely indeterminate, then at least the order is determined by the refusal and as its very gesture.[38]

It is the performance of another thinking of being with each other as citizens. These words circulate outside and beyond the imposed order of the camp. This is a refusal to submit to the order of power and to accept the way in which the order of law and the language of the law taxonomize the subject. As Leslie Hill has observed:

> Writing ... is always other than the law, not because of its superior power or legitimacy in the face of the law, but rather because of its refusal, on grounds of impotence, impossibility, and weakness, to allow itself to be addressed by the language of the law and constituted by the law as a subject or hostage of that law. ... [P]receding the discourse of law, lacking all unity, presence, and identity, writing is a challenge to any authority whatsoever, including of course its own.[39]

---

[36] Hannah Arendt, *The Human Condition* (Chicago, University of Chicago Press, 1998), 179.

[37] Jean-Luc Nancy, *The Birth To Presence* (Stanford: Stanford University Press, 1993), 308.

[38] Jean-Luc Nancy, *Multiple Arts: The Muses II* (Stanford: Stanford University Press, 2003), 17.

[39] Leslie Hill, *Maurice Blanchot: Extreme Contemporary* (London: Routledge, 1997), 187–8.

This characteristic of writing as a challenge to authority can be seen in the insubordination of language, a writing which refuses to be ordered. Thus, even in the necropolitical space of exception such words provide a means of performing a counter-power beyond the grasp of the appropriating hand of the state. What is at stake here is a politics which remains after the word has been written. The word survives as a witness to an impossible community. This is the self declaring itself not in response to the hailing or interpellation of the state or as the subject matter of law, but as an active participant in political affairs, a singularity which exceeds fixing. The poems are neither a declaration of war nor a retreat. They are an offer not an imposition, an invitation to a provisional relation without the violent backing of state force. It is the giving oneself over to an unknown other in the form of an appeal. These poems are not the marking of an end, the memorialization of a moment but rather an appeal addressed to another both absent yet present, to a time always already past and present. As such their writing performs the refusal of the appropriation of an ending. It is such an ephemeral writing of dissent that silently calls to a time beyond the political which leaves a stain on the presumed authority of the legal order. It is a demand for another politics, a politics beyond the time of the political, made not by inscribed and clearly delineated subjects of law, but of ghosts, traces, people without qualities, people without identity, whatever singularities.

I WISH TO THANK especially Julia Chryssostalis for her incisive comments on an earlier version of this piece.

— 8 —

On the Law of Originary Sociability *or* Writing the Law

Daniel Matthews

> One never writes alone.
>
> — J.-L. Nancy[1]

In December 1981 Jacques Derrida was arrested in Prague on charges of producing, trafficking, and transferring drugs. His arrest followed his involvement in an outlawed seminar with Czech dissident intellectuals organized by the Jan Hus Educational Foundation that sent books and hosted events in solidarity with those resisting the totalitarian policies of the then Czech government. At the time Derrida travelled to Prague, he was working on a text entitled *Préjugés: Devant la Loi*—'prejudices,' 'pre-judgement' or 'precedent' before the law—a text being prepared for a colloquium on Jean-François Lyotard. The events in Prague are alluded to in the later publication of 'Before the Law' in *Acts of Literature*.[2] Here Derrida mentions that his lawyer, appointed by the officials in Prague, said to him, 'You must feel that you are living a story by Kafka' and urged him, 'not to take [the situation] too tragically, live it as a literary experience.'[3] Charges were quickly dropped not,

---

[1] Jean-Luc Nancy, *The Inoperative Community* (Minneapolis: University of Minnesota Press, 2008), 73.

[2] Jacques Derrida, 'Before the Law,' in *Acts of Literature*, Derek Attridge ed. (Abingdon: Routledge, 2009), 181–220.

[3] Derrida, 'Before the Law,' 218.

however, before Derrida had been questioned for six or seven hours and spent a night in Ruzyne, Prague's prison.

Accounting for something of this 'literary' experience of the law—an experience perhaps all too real but still fantastic, darkly comic even—is central to Derrida's engagement with the law. Though his later 'Force of Law: The Mystical Foundation of Authority' has achieved canonical status within critical legal studies, it is perhaps the shorter intervention in 'Before the Law' in which we see more clearly Derrida's quiet admiration for the law, an appreciation for an immanent potential of the law. Where a necessary force and violence to the law is underscored in 'Force of Law,' it is a generative and poetic vein to which Derrida gestures in his reading of Kafka's *Vor dem Gesetz*. Kafka's vignette, capturing a sense of bewilderment and abandonment before the law, provides Derrida with the material to assess the common wellspring from which both law and literature emerge. For him, both discourses share the same conditions of possibility. They are both conditioned by a kind of 'non-origin,' an 'origin' that resists being finally located, determined, or defined. This refusal of origin is necessary for both literature and law. In our being denied access to the origin of law/literature, in our interminable suspension at their gates, in our abandonment, we experience what Derrida calls 'the law of the law,' a law common to both (positive) law and literature. This law of the law, for Derrida, is connected to an inchoate law of sociability. As he comments in *The Politics of Friendship*:

> We are caught up, one and another, in a sort of heteronomic and dissymmetrical curving of social space—more precisely, a curving of the relation to the other: prior to all organised *socius*, all *politeia*, all determined 'government,' *before* all 'law.' Prior to and before all law, in Kafka's sense of being 'before the law.' Let's get this right: prior to all *determined* law, *qua* natural law or positive law, but not law *in general*. For the heteronomic and dissymmetrical curving of a law of originary sociability is also a law, perhaps the very essence of law.[4]

In the following pages, I assess this 'law of originary sociability' by putting Derrida in conversation with Jean-Luc Nancy's notion of 'literary communism.' Both Nancy and Derrida see a potential in 'literature' and 'writing' to reveal a sense of this 'law' of a bare

---

[4] Jacques Derrida, *The Politics of Friendship* (London: Verso, 2005), 231.

and primary sociality to our being. By exploring a sense of 'writing' as that which exposes this prior law of sociability, I suggest that we might develop practices and modes of legal critique that interrupt the positive law's calculating proscriptions. 'Writing' the law, then, involves opening the positive law to this more primary law of sociability.

The Law Before the Law and Literary Communism

Kafka's parable *Vor dem Gesetz*, first published in 1915 in its own right, forms part of *The Trial* where it is recounted to Joseph K by a priest as K tours a cathedral.[5] As is well known, the story tells of a man from the country who seeks admittance to the law (*das Gesetz*). Before the law stands a doorkeeper, attending a gate that stands open, as usual. The countryman heeds the doorkeeper's advice to defer entry 'at the moment,' hoping that the veto will be lifted in the future. Such difficulties the man did not expect as he thought that the law was accessible at all times, to everyone. The man's waiting continues for years throughout which time he begs the doorkeeper for admittance. He offers all his possessions to bribe the doorkeeper and even, in his childlike old age, begs the fleas on the doorkeeper's collar for help in his cause. The countryman's final request is to know why for all the years that he has waited for admittance no one else has ever sought entry to the law. The doorkeeper bends down to roar in the man's ear: 'No one else could ever be admitted here, since this gate was made only for you. I am now going to shut it.'[6]

---

[5] The priest claims that the story is taken from 'the writings that preface the Law' and suggests that the tale illustrates K's delusion about the nature of the court. See F. Kafka, *The Trial*, trans. Willa Muir and Edwin Muir (London: Everyman's Library, 1992), 234–6. The chaplain who is the first to interpret Kafka's tale turns out to be the prison chaplain and therefore a member of the court and in cahoots with the law.

[6] Franz Kafka, 'Before the Law' in *The Complete Short Stories of Franz Kafka* (London: Vintage, 1999), 3–4. Kafka's tale has extensively referenced within critical legal studies and the philosophy of law. I have found the following particularly helpful: Costas Douzinas and Adam Gearey, *Critical Jurisprudence* (Oxford: Hart Publishing, 2005), 336–362; Elena Loizidou, 'Before the Law, encounters at the borderline' in *New Critical Legal Thinking*, eds. Matthew Stone, Illan Rua Wall, and Costas Douzinas (Abingdon: Routledge, 2012), 181–97; Hélène Cixous, *Readings: The Poetics of Blanchot, Joyce, Kafka, Kleist, Lispector, and Tsvetayeva* (Minneapolis: University of Minnesota Press, 1991), 14–19; Jacques de Ville, 'Before the Law' in *Jacques Derrida: Law as Absolute Hospitality* (London: Routledge, 2011), 74–94; George Dargo, 'Reclaiming Franz Kafka, Doctor of Jurisprudence' *Brandies Law Journal* 45/3 (2006–7), 495; Giorgio

One of the tropes that has produced much comment is the confrontation in the story between the singularity of the man who comes before the law and the generality of the law that he encounters. This is made all the clearer by the man's humble origins as a 'man from the country' and the generality of *Gesetz*, referring to law in general rather than particular laws (*Recht*), that confronts him. The failure of the countryman to access the law is a constitutive failure of the law to be just with the singularity of those that appear before it. Whilst this analysis forms part of Derrida's reading of the text, his focus is on the countryman's ultimately failed attempt to locate the origin of the law. In exploring this ineluctable desire to enter the law, Derrida puts Kafka's story in conversation with Freud's fable of the founding of the moral law in *Totem and Taboo*. Freud's own narrative is dictated, likewise, by a certain failure: in an effort to fix and determine the origin of the law and identify a stable and transcendental referent about which the law can orientate, Freud manifestly fails. As Derrida comments, Freud's fable recounts a 'non-event' where nothing happens, no (transcendental) origin is located.[7] As Peter Fitzpatrick has argued, the power of Freud's myth of foundation is to reveal the impossibility of maintaining a stable origin and the efficacy of Freud's tale is to put modern law's grounds in question. This failure to locate the law's origin 'proves to be a productive failure' that exposes a non-transcendental referent at the heart of the law.[8] It is this prior work before the law that Derrida explores in his reading of Kafka and Freud.

As indicated at the outset, in Derrida's account, the law and literature share the same conditions of possibility. Kafka's tale of the man from the country and Freud's myth of the foundation of the moral law in *Totem and Taboo* show that the lawfulness of law (the law of the law) and the literariness of literature are both conditioned by a certain aporia or undecidiability. I want to stress *showing* here because it is precisely in what these two 'literary texts' *show* rather than *tell* that, I think, is crucial for

Agamben, *Homo Sacer: Sovereign Power and Bare Life* (Stanford: Stanford University Press, 1998), 49–62.
    [7] Derrida, 'Before the Law,' 199.
    [8] Peter Fitzpatrick, *Modernism and the Grounds of Law* (Cambridge: Cambridge University Press, 2001), 12.

Derrida.⁹ Both stories in Derrida's reading are strange non-events, they are relations or stories where nothing really happens. The murder of the primordial father in Freud's fable of the origin of the law is only effective because of the guilt that the sons feel. The supposed founding event of the law, then, must depend on a prior moral law that enables the sons to feel guilt and remorse. Furthermore, in the institution of the prohibition of murder and incest, the very things that the sons desire before the murder—the father's power over the community—is maintained from beyond the grave. Though an 'event,' the effects are hardly discernible. Derrida suggests that this is a tale that tells of 'an event without event, pure event where nothing happens.'¹⁰ Kafka's tale of the man who seeks admittance to the law, similarly tells of a manifest failure. Just like Freud in his attempt to find the origin of the law, the man from the country is unable to reach the law; he cannot even come close, he is stymied by the first of what we are told are many doorkeepers. What both Freud and Kafka show is the impossibility of access to the origin of the law and in so doing both reveal a certain space 'before' or prior to the law as the law's condition of possibility. This failure to tell of the access to the law itself is conditioned by *différance*, a perpetual play of difference and deferral. That the law cannot itself be approached or determined is the law of the law. As Derrida says:

> What is deferred forever till death is entry into the law itself, which is nothing other than that which dictates the delay... . What *must not* and *cannot* be approached is the origin of *différance*: it must

---

⁹ I take this sense of 'showing' rather than 'telling' or 'saying' from Ludwig Wittgenstein, *Tractatus Logico Philosophicus*, trans. C. K. Ogden (London: Routledge, 2005), 5.62: 'what solipsism *means* is quite correct, only it cannot be *said*, but it *shows* itself' and at 2.172 'the picture... cannot represent its form of representation; it shows it forth.' A not dissimilar distinction is made by Benjamin who describes his method in the *Arcades Project* as 'literary montage'; he suggests that he 'needn't say anything, merely *show*'; See Walter Benjamin, *The Arcades Project*, trans. H. Eiland (New York: Belknap Press, 2002), 1, n. 2. The notion that I want to pursue here is that a 'sense' or 'meaning' is revealed that something is said or presented, irrespective of that saying's content. To emphasize 'showing' in the present context is to underscore the extent to which both Kafka and Freud reveal a sense of the origin of the law without being able to render that origin into a definable or presentable 'saying' or formula. Echoing Fitzpatrick's discussion of Freud's 'productive failure' to locate the origin of the law in *Totem and Taboo*, we might suggest that Freud's failing to 'tell' the origin of the law nonetheless allows him to 'show' such an (non-)origin; see n. 8.

¹⁰ Derrida, 'Before the Law,' 199.

not be presented or represented and above all not penetrated. That is the law of the law, the process of a law of whose subject we can never say, 'There it is,' it is here or there.[11]

Freud's text in particular, is driven by a desire to narrate the origins of the law but this narration itself annuls or interrupts the myth of the law's origin. We are left with nothing but this non-event where no origin is revealed.

Yet it is precisely in this relation of a 'non-event' that something is shown. That which instigates Freud's failure to tell us of the origin of the law is also the very condition of the man from the country who is held in check at the law's outermost threshold. Both texts describe a certain aporetic experience of being before—as in, up in front of—the law. And this is the very same condition of being before a literary text. It is the literariness of these two texts that enables them to *show* the impossibility of accessing the law's origin or condition of possibility. The literary text holds us in a certain state of non-knowing, of undecidability or aporia between readability and unreadability and this condition is precisely the condition of being before the law.[12]

In Kafka's tale, the law (*das Gesetz*) is unknown, it is rendered in the neuter gender and so cannot even be given a feminine or masculine identity. As Derrida says, 'we neither know *who* nor *what* is the law.' And it is in this space of non-knowing, Derrida suggests, 'where literature begins.'[13] Literature becomes a witness to the law's non-origin: it is able to *show* the law's *différance*. Literature performs the deferral that Kafka's tale relates, the potency of literature is located in the fact that it depends on this very deferral for its efficacy. Our encounter with literature must take place between the readable and unreadable, the translatable and untranslatable, the knowable and unknowable: literature holds us at the threshold of these two poles. Significantly, the play between these poles is constitutive of the medium itself. The literariness of literature is revealed in its ability to resist becoming totally transparent, its very 'essence' is in its ability to escape any crude essentialism. This fact endows literature with privileged capacities to precisely *show*, in its resistance to final determination, that which makes the law, the

---

[11] Derrida, 'Before the Law,' 205.   [12] Derrida, 'Before the Law,' 196.
[13] Derrida, 'Before the Law,' 207.

law. And it is precisely this resistance to any final determination that is the law of the law and the law of literature.

In a similar way to Derrida's privileging of literature or the 'literariness of literature' in the task of exposing the condition of possibility of the law, Nancy's notion of 'literary communism,' developed in *The Inoperative Community*, privileges literature's ability to expose the ontological register of 'being singular plural.' For Nancy, the potential of 'literature' or 'writing' lies in its ability to interrupt or suspend myths of foundation, totality, or closure. 'Literature' or 'writing' cannot sustain a singular self. The written, narrational, or authorial 'I' is already split and necessarily open to otherness. Even if one writes for oneself, the 'I' to whom one writes is already separated from the 'I' who, at the very moment of inscription, pens a phrase, a poem, or a shopping list.[14] This necessary openness to otherness will always exceed and interrupt attempts to delimit and define. Writing, perhaps most clear in a literary or poetic mode, draws its effect from its very instability, the open potential for a plurality of inferences and meanings. It is writing's capacity obliquely to express—or *show* rather than *tell*—that lends it a certain affinity with Nancy's ontology. Nancy's 'literary communism' does not suggest that certain literary forms or tropes tell of being singular plural, rather Nancy suggests that in literature or writing being-in-common as being singular plural shows itself. As Nancy suggests:

> Being-in-common is literary, that is, if we can attempt to say that it has its very being in 'literature' ... then what 'literature' will have to designate is this being itself... in itself. In other words, it would designate that singular ontological quality that gives being in common, that does not hold it in reserve, before or after community, as an essence ... but that rather makes for a being that is only when shared in common.[15]

'Literature,' in the sense outlined here, exposes a certain originary law of being social. In its suspension and interruption of myths of presence, fixed identities, or determinate meaning, literature shows the being-in-common as that which will necessarily precede such

---

[14] On the connection between writing (or iterability) and a fundamental troubling of identity, see Jacques Derrida, 'Signature, Event, Context,' in *Limited Inc.* ed. G. Graff (Evanston: Northwestern University Press, 1988), 49.

[15] Nancy, *Inoperative Community*, 64.

identities and meanings and in so doing disrupt and displace them.

Returning to Derrida's reading of 'Before the Law,' through the lens of Nancy's take on literature and writing, we can perhaps get a sense of a certain connection between the law before the law and the sense of 'being social' that animates the present collection. Writing resists the law. In its necessary ability to transgress, always to point outside or elsewhere, writing exceeds and undermines the law's efforts to determine and delimit. But so too does writing reveal another law. A law of being-in-common, of sharing in a common exposure to alterity at the limit of singular selves. It is in writing or literature that we find resources for resistance or insubordination in the face of the law but so too do we find another poetics of the law, a law of originary sociability that is both without foundation or discernible *telos*.

Perhaps it is this alternative poetics of sociability before the law to which Derrida and Nancy both point in their reliance on 'literature.' As Leslie Hill notes, writing of Maurice Blanchot's take on the relation between law and literature, 'lacking all unity, presence and identity, writing is a challenge to any authority whatsoever, including of course its own.'[16] It is this 'weak force' of literature to which Derrida briefly alludes when discussing his own experience of being before the law in Prague. Upon his return to France, Derrida was interviewed about his experiences for a television programme but he felt immediately stymied by the medium. He later reflected that, 'what I really lived through… would demand a different form of narration, another poetics than that of the evening news.'[17] Perhaps it is towards this, then, that Nancy and Derrida urge us on the question of sociability before the law: to think and to write a different poetics of being social and, consequently, a different poetics of the law.

Writing the Law: Strategies for Critical Legal Praxis

The notion of an immanent potential within the law —the sense of an 'other law' inhering but exceeding positive law—has preoccupied post-structural accounts of legality. From Derrida's assertion

---

[16] Leslie Hill, *Maurice Blanchot: Extreme Contemporary* (London: Routledge, 1997), 188.

[17] Quoted in Catherine Malabou and Jacques Derrida, *Counterpath: Travelling with Jacques Derrida* (Standford: Stanford University Press, 2004), 174.

that deconstruction 'is the Law ... an affirmation on the side of the Law,'[18] to the desire, articulated in the 'Force of Law,' to 'reserve the possibility of ... a law that not only exceeds or contradicts law but also ... has no relation to law or maintains such a strange relation to it that it may just as well demand law as exclude it,'[19] post-structural thought has always held onto the possibility of a 'law' beyond the realm of state sanction. For Nancy, such a 'law' is associated with a 'law of abandonment,' a law by which self and other are primarily implicated by the bare fact of our being in the world.[20] In Blanchot and Foucault, we get something similar with both thinkers asserting an other law within the law, a law of the outside that nonetheless haunts the interiority.[21] The law, in such a reading, takes on a doubled sense of law as both positive and violent, but also indeterminable and open. Such an account of the law retains the possibility of opening up the law to new vistas and possibilities. As Fitzpatrick suggests, the absence of a fully determinate content to the law calls for 'the responsive opening of that content to the possibility of being otherwise.'[22] But what is often less clearly articulated, in such accounts, are the strategies by which such an opening might be effected. If we seek to follow Derrida and Nancy's evocation of a poetics of the law that exposes our originary sociality, what form might such a poetics take?

Here, I want to briefly touch on what I see to be the strategies through which such openings within the law might be possible. This first involves an attentiveness to the law's expressive register, suggesting that in occupying certain legal techniques and practices we might 'write' the law otherwise.

For Nancy, the 'writing' which exposes being-in-common is not limited to visible marks or inscriptions on a page. 'Writing' refers to a series of practices by which the serous and inoperative 'being-with' that is the cornerstone of his philosophy is revealed. As he

---

[18] Jacques Derrida, 'Women in the Beehive: A Seminar with Jacques Derrida,' *Differences: A Journal of Feminist Cultural Studies* 16/3 (2005), 149.

[19] Derrida, 'Force of Law,' 233.

[20] Jean-Luc Nancy, 'Abandoned Being' in *The Birth to Presence*, trans. Brian Holmes (Stanford: Stanford University Press, 1993).

[21] See Maurice Blanchot, *The Unavowable Community*, trans. Pierre Jorris (New York: Station Hill, 1988), 24–26 and Michel Foucault, 'Maurice Blanchot: The Thought from Outside' (London: Zone Books, 1990), 7–58.

[22] Peter Fitzpatrick, 'Juris-fiction: Literature and the Law of the Law' *Ariel: A Review of International English Literature* 35/1–2 (2004), 225.

suggests, 'writing' or 'literature' refers broadly to 'writing ... voice ... music, dance, the exercise of thought.'[23] The list, one imagines, might be endless; we might attach the name 'writing' to any practice that works to interrupt narratives of closure and identity and expose a more originary sense of an inoperative being-in-common. In privileging an expanded category of 'writing,' Nancy is following Derrida and Blanchot who both use the term to refer to a sense of excessive difference that at once marks the conditions of possibility for signification and signification's constitutive failure.[24] As is well known, in the *Grammatology*, Derrida uses 'writing' (or arche-writing, *écriture*) to refer to a movement of difference and deferral that is prior to speech. Where speech is commonly tied to presence—supposedly conveying the *present* thoughts of a *present* subject—for Derrida, writing, with its connection to absence, spatial difference and temporal deferral, comes to name the movement that escapes metaphysical determinations founded on an economy of presence. Nancy's literary communism reads a political significance into this understanding of 'writing.' Rather than dwell on textual play, Nancy suggests that our political ontology is shaped by a sense of 'writing,' proposing that our bare sociality (the mere fact of our being-with others in the world) is conditioned by something 'writerly' in the sense that efforts to fix and determine our social relations are always undercut by a prior movement of difference. The free play that holds metaphysical assertions of the 'subject,' 'author' or 'truth' in suspense, also conditions our political and social networks. Nancy's reliance on 'writing,' then, must be understood within this post-structural heritage.[25] I want to

[23] Nancy, *Inoperative Community*, 64.

[24] On Blanchot's account of writing, see Maurice Blanchot, 'Literature and the Right to Death' in *The Work of Fire*, trans. Charlotte Mandell (Stanford: Stanford University Press, 1995), 300–344. Blanchot here writes against Jean-Paul Sartre's notion of 'engaged literature,' suggesting that writing's power comes from its ambiguous and doubly negated relation to the world. And for Derrida's seminal account see Jacques Derrida, *Of Grammatology*, trans. Gayatri Spivak (Baltimore: Johns Hopkins University Press, 1997).

[25] My privileging of 'writing' follows the sense of the term briefly laid out here. I am not unaware of the baggage associate with such a choice. A common concern with deconstruction lies in the privileging of the textual over the material, the scriptural over the oral, and the literary over the political. These worries, directly associated with the privileging of 'writing' are, in part, undeniable. However, it is precisely the (re)inscription of the textual and poetic into the political and material that Nancy's account of 'literary communism' seeks to achieve. It is in this vein, and in keeping with an established deconstructive usage of 'writing,' that I retain the signifier.

suggest that practices of 'writing' (so understood) can be fruitfully deployed within a legal context to counter myths of the presence and orderliness of the law and expose, instead, the inchoate law of sociality discussed above. It is through such practices that we might privilege a post-structural 'law of being social' over the positive law's exacting calculations.

Such practices of 'writing,' I want to suggest, can be most effectively deployed within the register of jurisdiction. Jurisdiction is commonly conceived as a technical and administrative contrivance, the preserve of black letter lawyers and forensic technocrats. A quick skim of any introductory text on the conflict of laws will soon confirm this prejudice. However, jurisdiction is also the expressive register of the law, it names practices for declaring, showing, and determining the limits and possibilities of legality. *Juris-diction* is the 'speaking of the law,' the performative and representational mode of normativity.[26] In a variety of practices and procedures, jurisdiction allows the law to be known and understood. Perhaps, then, in this expressive dimension of the law we might see possibilities for 'writing' the law otherwise.

The jurisdictional moment *par excellence* is the constitutional declaration in which a community comes together to assert their legal and political presence and integrity. In classical constitutionalism, this authority to speak the law in the name of the community rests with 'constituent power.' This power is ultimately orientated towards the establishment of a new constitutional order and thus has as its *telos* constituted power; that is, the power over a particular polity, invested in a constitutional document or the institutions and practices of the state. Constituent power, in the classical mould, is wedded to identity and essentialism, taking shape in the 'people' or 'nation' that, when evoked, has the power to topple constituted power in the name of the higher authority that it purports to represent. The essentialism and teleological orientation of classical

---

[26] A small but growing body of critical literature on jurisdiction assesses jurisdiction in this mode. See, in particular, Edward Mussawir, *Jurisdiction in Deleuze: The Expression and Representation of Law* (Abingdon: Routledge, 2011); Shannaugh Dorsett and Shaun McVeigh, *Jurisdiction* (Abingdon: Routledge, 2012); Bradin Cormack, *A Power to do Justice: Jurisdiction, English Literature and the Rise of the Common Law 1509–1625* (Chicago, IL: Chicago University Press, 2007); and Shaun McVeigh, ed., *Jurisprudence of Jurisdiction*, (Abingdon: Routledge, 2007). Jurisdiction, conceived as the law's expressive register would encompass, judgments, cartographic representations of legal space, constitutional declarations, rules governing court procedure and so on.

constituent power is clearly anathema to the 'writing' towards which Nancy gestures. The power of 'writing' lies in its capacity to interrupt the closure that constituent power enacts. However, might we hold open the possibility of 'writing' constituent power and imagining this jurisdictional practice otherwise?

The anxieties that animate this question have been carefully examined by Illan rua Wall, who—in seeking to free constituent power from its metaphysical forms—has developed an account of 'open constituent power.'[27] Drawing on Nancy, Rancière, Agamben et al., Wall argues that the power of constituent power lies precisely in the fact that it exceeds the identitarian and essentialist logic commonly associated with the principle. Open constituent power does not claim some transcendent ground for its praxis, nor does it have constituted power as its ultimate goal. Rather, it is argued that constituent power rests on an inoperative 'being-with' that cannot be fully determined or captured. And rather than seeking *potestas* (the power over something), constituent power should be conceived as an expression of open *potentia* (the power, or potential, to do something). Constituent power, in Wall's formulation, is a strategic and temporary opening of possibility within the polity and, as a jurisdictional moment, the expression of constituent power should be understood as an interruption of the closure and presence instantiated by positive law.

Significantly, for our present purposes, Wall ties this sense of the open potential of constituent power to the notion of 'righting.'[28] Not only homophonic with the 'writing' which preoccupies Nancy and Derrida, 'righting' is also substantively imbricated with a practice of 'writing' which exposes monadic selves to an originary otherness. Costas Douzinas, the first to coin the term, connects 'righting' to the potential of a non-metaphysical humanism that re-awakens and transforms the social bond. Douzinas argues that such a reanimation of our sociality involves shifting the parameters of our understanding of (human) rights away from the liberal

---

[27] Illan rua Wall, *Human Rights and Constituent Power: Without Model or Warranty* (Abingdon: Routledge, 2012); Illan rua Wall, 'Notes on an "Open" Constituent Power,' *Law Culture and the Humanities* (forthcoming), available online before print, accessed 8 March 2014, doi: 10.1177/1743872113501840; Illan rua Wall, 'Tunisia and the Critical Legal Theory of Dissensus,' *Law and Critique* 23/3 (2012), 219–36.

[28] Wall, *Human Rights and Constituent Power*, 133–46. Wall himself notes a connection between righting and writing, see 180, n. 53.

individualism most commonly associated with the discourse. As he suggests:

> Some human rights may be consistent with non-metaphysical humanism. But the overall form of the social bond would change from rights and principles to being-in-common, to the public recognition and protection of the becoming-human with others, a dynamic process which resists all attempts to hold humanity to an essence decided by the representatives of power. To coin a term, this would be a process of 'righting' and not a series of rights and, like writing, it would open Being to the new and unknown as a condition of its humanity.[29]

Righting is thus an immanent potential within rights but nonetheless a task that requires creative praxis and intervention. Such interventions that seek to 'right' rights, however, do not assert some essential or transcendental 'truth' or create new or higher order rights, rather they would involve practices that trouble such closures, allowing, instead, for the coming of a non-metaphysical and anti-foundationalist sense of being-in-common.

As intimated above, I want to suggest that such interventions can most effectively be made through the strategic occupation of the law's jurisdictional function. By co-opting the law's expressive dimension and righting/writing the law otherwise, we might expose the immanent but dormant 'other law within the law'—the law of sociality or being-with—that animates the post-structural account of legality.

The occupations of the squares and public spaces in early 2011 perhaps give us the clearest sense of this process of writing/righting the law. These movements—though clearly situated in singular circumstances, owing their effectiveness (or lack thereof) to the particular claims made in each instance as well as the existing local political dynamics—were united, we might say, in their common disunity. In each case, from Tahrir to Syntagma, Zuccotti Park to the *Indignados* of Madrid, these movements disavowed established parties and firm groupings, expressing instead the open potential of people coming together to demand change. Reflecting on the occupation of Syntagma Square, Douzinas notes that: 'a motley

---

[29] Costas Douzinas, *The End of Human Rights* (Oxford: Hart Publishing, 2000), 215–216. Quoted in Wall, *Human Rights and Constituent Power*, 145.

multitude of indignant men and women of all ideologies, races and occupations, including the many unemployed... came from all parties and none.'[30] These participants belonged without belonging to an identity, they appropriated belonging itself in their act of coming together. As Wall suggests of the protest and resistance in Tunisia, 'there was no *condition* of belonging to the protests.'[31] There was no pre-determined identity to which participants had to conform, no party or ethnicity of which one had to be a member.[32]

These events 'wrote' the law. The law's claim to represent the people and speak with the authority of the community was co-opted by the 'motley crews' that gathered in the squares. These gatherings were jurisdictional in nature. But they did not declare or announce the positive law, sign a constitutional text, or delimit the scope of the community's authority; rather, a different 'law' was written. In embracing difference and deferring teleological commitments to (constituted) power, these events—as much of the journalistic coverage at the time testified[33]—hovered between the readable and the unreadable, deriving their force from a resistance to final determination and definition. In this sense, these events were 'writing/righting' the law, exposing another law, a 'law' of a more primary, but inchoate, sense of sociability, that, as Derrida reminds us, 'is perhaps the very essence of the law.'

There is, perhaps, a danger here of romanticisation. This more primary 'law of sociability' that was written in the streets and in the squares cannot, in itself, secure the political, economic, and moral conditions for which those present campaigned. Such rights and duties ultimately depend on the positive law's determinative capacity for enforcement. Nonetheless, the power of these events, it seems to me, lies in their capacity, through intervention, occupation, and praxis, to show the *différantial* law before the law that Derrida identifies in relation to Kafka and Freud. Derrida's reading above

---

[30] Costas Douzinas, '*Stasis Syntagma*: The Names and Types of Resistance,' in Stone, Wall, and Douzinas, *New Critical Legal Thinking*, 40.

[31] Illan rua Wall, 'A Different Constituent Power: Agamben and Tunisia,' in Stone, Wall, and Douzinas, *New Critical Legal Thinking*, 64, 61–6.

[32] Wall contrasts this with the situation in Libya where the resistance against Gaddafi was quickly racialized where 'darker skinned' inhabitants were expelled or executed, blamed for being mercenaries. See Wall, 'A Different Constituent Power,' 64.

[33] As Douzinas notes, the uprisings in 2011 were largely unforeseen by the media and when they did arrive were greeted with bewilderment. See Costas Douzinas, *Philosophy and Resistance in the* Crisis (London: Polity, 2013), 1–15.

suggested that for the positive law to have effects, there must be a prior 'law' at work. The events of early 2011, understood as practices of 'writing,' showed, in an act of creation, this law of sociability.

Taking these events as our cue, I would venture that critical legal scholarship needs to engage, theorize, highlight and animate such practices of 'writing the law.' The site of such interventions might, most productively, be found in law's expressive register, in those practices that represent the law's presence and scope. Such practices might be found in: visual representations, other than traditional cartographic forms, that express legal space or the effects of the imposition of normative orders;[34] in the interruption of courtroom procedure that seeks to silence the voice of those who appear before the court;[35] or in the re-writing of judicial decisions and pronouncements.[36] In every case, through an occupation of, and intervention within, the law's jurisdictional register, 'writing' would be a strategy of creative practice that seeks to expose an 'other law' always already at work within the putative rigidity of the extant legal form. Such a 'writing' of the law would seek to expose a more fundamental 'law' that comes before the law, a law of sharing and fracture, through which self and other are always already co-implicated. Such practices, rather than simply holding open the promise or potential of opening the law otherwise, seek, through creative praxis and intervention, to right the (positive) law by writing this law of sociability anew.

---

[34] For a comparative analysis of two systems of visually representing legal space, see Shannaugh Dorsett, 'Mapping Territories' in McVeigh, *Jurisprudence of Jurisdiction*, 137–58.

[35] For an assessment of Maurice Blanchot's own disruption of court procedure or a 'writing of the law otherwise' see Patrick Hanafin, 'The Writer's Refusal and the Law's Malady,' *Journal of Law and Society* 31/1 (2004), 6.

[36] For such an effort, see Rosemary Hunter, Clare McGlynn and Erika Rackley, eds., *Feminist Judgments: From Theory to Practice* (Oxford: Hart Publishing, 2010). It should be noted that this project embraces, rather than challenges, the extant common law form of judgment. Nonetheless, in re-writing existing judgments with an eye to feminist theoretical and political concerns, the contributors open a space of contingency within the law, illustrating how the law might be reimagined otherwise. Though not explicitly alluding to an ontology of 'being-with,' the project demonstrates the critical potential in occupying and recasting the jurisdictional register of legality.

Index

Agamben 109
Agamben, Giorgio 109
AIDS 77, 79, 80, 83, 84–6
alterity 10, 37, 121
Anzaldua, Gloria 78, 79, 81
Aquinas, Thomas 3
Arendt, Hannah 3, 111–2
Aristotle 3

Balibar, Étienne 107
Bataille, Georges
    community 82
    contestation of knowledge 89
    death 86
biopower 105, 109. *See also* Foucault, Michel: biopower/ disciplinary power
Blanchot, Maurice
    autrui 105
    community 7
    experience of birth/death 83
    death 86
    law and literature 121
    other law within the law 122
    transcendent, illimitable law 41
    unavowable community 6–7, 76
    writing 123
Butler, Judith 11, 101
    category of women 81
    poems from Guantanamo 106–9
    poetic sociality 102
    Queer Nation 79
    queer theory 80
    the term 'queer' 88

The Creation of the World or Globalization. Nancy, Jean-Luc 54, 62
citizen
    as object of governance 103–4
    empty figure of 65
    exemplar 63
    formal presentation of demos 64
    good and/or failed 93–4, 99
    response to biopower 105
    versus migrant 98
    workers 95
Coetzee, J. M. 105
community. *See also* Blanchot: community; *See also* Nancy, Jean-Luc: community; *See also* poststructural: thought: of community
    as being with others 104. *See also* Nancy, Jean-Luc: mitsein/being with
    as experience of death 82, 87. *See also* death
    cooptation by law 127
    displacement 81
    shared value 94, 97
    singular plural 66
    textual illusion of 108
    unavowable 6, 76, 110
    unworked/inoperative 64, 111
constitutionalism 124
    constituent power 124–5
    constituted power 124, 125, 127
    potestas & *potentia* 125
Critique of Judgement. Kant, Immanuel. 19
Crowley, Martin 29, 30–1
death. *See also* god: death of; *See also* Blanchot: death; *See also* Derrida: what is deferred forever till death
    and queer politics 79–80, 85, 86
    and the political 77
    as basis of sociality 76
    as experience of singular finitude 82–83. *See also* Nancy, Jean-Luc: finitude
    poem. *See* al-Dossari, Jumah

deconstruction 88, 122

practices of 2
democracy. *See also* Derrida:
    democracy to come; *See*
    also Gezi Park protest
    direct 75
    real 75
Derrida, Jacques. *See also* law: before
    the law (Kafka): Derrida's
    reading of; *See also* law:
    of originary sociability
    arrested 114
    democracy 63
      to come 9
    différance 118, 119
    essence of the law 127
    force of law 115, 122
    hospitality 43, 63
    law of the law 115
    politics of friendship 115
    deferred forever till death 118–9
    writing 123, 125
al-Dossari, Jumah 109–110
Douzinas, Costas 125–6

The Experience of Freedom. Nancy,
    Jean-Luc 27–30
Esposito, Roberto 110
ethics 30–31

'The Forgetting of Philosophy.'
    Nancy, Jean-Luc 47
Falkoff, Marc 102–103
Finlay, Christoper 18
Fitzpatrick, Peter 10, 12, 117, 118, 122
Foucault, Michel 5, 40, 80
    biopower/disciplinary
      power 37, 41, 44
    governmentality 33–35
foundation
    anti- 126
    in Hume and Kant 17–21
    post- 8
    self- 23
    un-ground 23
    withdrawal of 20–2

Gezi Park protest 70–2. *See also* peace
    pianist; *See also* standing man
god. *See also* Rousseau, Jean-Jacques
    creation without 51
    death of 36–7. *See*
      also Nietzsche, Friedrich

hermeneutics 48
tatters of worn-out finery 100
world without 65
governmentality 33–5, 37
Gündüz, Erdem. *See* standing man:

Hanafin, Patrick 13
Heidegger, Martin 31, 36–7, 50.
    See also Nancy, Jean-Luc:
    influence of: Heidegger
    Geworfenheit 9
    Hermeneutics 48
    ontological difference 49
human. *See also* Nancy, Jean-Luc:
    human, non-human
    homo sapiens 29
    humanity 19, 20, 63
    image of 17, 21, 31
    nature 17–21, 29. *See*
      also Hume, David
    sociability 18, 19
Hume, David 21, 28
Hutchens, Benjamin 31

identity
    categories of 85, 87
    challenging the imposition of 104
    constitutent power 124
    disavowel of categories of 77
    disclosure of 52
    essentialized 2
    group 92
    interruption of 123
    of the demos 64
    opposed by poetic sociality 111
    politics of 78
    process of differentiation 66
    protection of 91
    sexual 80
    unworking of 87
    with itself 63
    without belonging 127
    without essence 88
Inoperative Community. Nancy,
    Jean-Luc 76
inoperativity 11, 83. *See also* Nancy,
    Jean-Luc: inopera-
    tive: as resistance
justice. *See also* Nancy, Jean-Luc: justice
    beyond the law 108–110
    coming of the other 45
    impossible 109

INDEX

Kant, Immanuel 25–6, 28, 30
   in Nancy 22–5
   sociability, human nature,
      judgement 19–20, 21
labour
   and migration 90–100
   precariousness 95
Lacoue-Labarthe, Philippe 3, 11, 62
Laruelle, François 21
law. *See also* community: textual illusion of; *See also* poetry: against the law; *See also* Derrida: essence of the law; *See also* Derrida: force of law; *See also* Derrida: law of the law
   before the law (Kafka) 115–119
      Derrida's reading
         of 117–119
   fiction 45
   illimitability 41. *See also* law: responsiveness
   of originary sociability 42, 114–28
   other law 121, 122, 126, 128. *See also* alterity
   responsiveness 39–40, 44. *See also* Nonet, Philippe and Selznick, Philip
   words beyond 108–111
   writing/righting 121–28
Lefort, Claude 8, 35
Levinas, Emmanuel 31

Malabou, Catherine 11
Martello, Davide. *See* Gezi Park protest: peace pianist
Marx, Karl 5
   11th Thesis 56
   Marxist. *See* Pashukanis, Evgeny
Matthews, Daniel 13
Meurs, Pieter & Devisch, Ignaas 6, 12, 98
migrant
   connotation 95
   labour. *See* Labour and Migration
militant erotic interventions 79–80
Morin, Marie-Eve 13
Mulqueen, Tara 13

Nancy, Jean-Luc. *See also* Kant, Immanuel: in Nancy
   abandonment 9, 10
   Abyss, Freedom, Relation 22–8

anxiety of social being 1, 2
being 49. *See also* Nancy, Jean-Luc: sense; *See also* Nancy, Jean-Luc: mitsein/being with in-common 67–9. *See also* Nancy, Jean-Luc: mitsein/being with; *See also* Nancy, Jean-Luc: the (k)not
   law of 121
   literary 104, 120
   writing 104
community 11, 31
Darstellung 23
death 83–4
democracy 61–75
   demos 63–7
ecotechnics 61–2, 64
experience of freedom 26–30
exscription 53, 96–7
finitude 84
   politics of 31
globalization 54–7
ground(lessness) of being social 26, 30–2
human, non-human 28–30. *See also* Hume, David
influence of
   Derrida 22
   Heidegger 22, 24–5
   Nietzsche 22
inoperative 76–7, 83
   as resistance 87–8, 105
   community 7, 64, 82, 104–5
jurisdiction 24, 124
justice 30–1
lapsus judicii 23–4
limit of philosophy 27
literary communism 115–120
mitsein/being with 6, 7
(non-) foundation 26, 31. *See also* foundation: self-; *See also* foundation: un-ground; *See also* foundation: withdrawal of
poetry 112
politics 31, 68
prominence of 11
sense 6, 90–91, 98–100
   See also Nancy, Jean-Luc: globalization (and) being 49–50
   meaning of 47–57
   of the world 50–2

touching the world 52–4
singular plural 28, 31, 63–9. *See also* community: singular plural
sociality. *See* sociality: renewed thinking of (in Nancy)
society 7
sovereignty 81
the (k)not 10. *See also* Nancy, Jean-Luc: being: in-common; *See also* Nancy, Jean-Luc: mitsein/being with
theologico-political 65
the political 3, 11
transimmanence 12, 65
unworked community. *See* Nancy, Jean-Luc: inoperative community
writing
 and being 104
 the law 121–8
nation state 36, 37, 44, 92, 93, 94, 97, 98, 99
neoliberal
 economies 33
 -ism 97
 -ization 97–8
 modernity 105
 society 39
Nietzsche, Friedrich 22, 35–7. *See also* god: death of
Nisancioglu, Kerem 74
Nonet, Philippe and Selznick, Philip 39–40

ontological imperative 56
ontology
 absence of ground 31
 being singular plural 11, 27, 28. *See also* Nancy, Jean-Luc: singular plural
 bodily 91
 in Nancy 22. *See also* Nancy, Jean-Luc: being
 political 123
 re-invention of ontological vocabulary 47
otherness 120, 125. *See* alterity

Pashukanis, Evgeny 39
peace pianist 70–2. *See also* Gezi Park protest
Plato 3
Poems from Guantanamo: The Detainees Speak. Butler, Judith 102
poetry 101–13. *See also* Butler: poems from Guantanamo; *See also* justice: impossible against the law 104–8
 as life into truthful form 106
 as originary sociality 107
 as resistance 112. *See also* Nancy, Jean-Luc: inoperative: as resistance
 unauthorized 109
the political 3, 113, 123. *See also* Lacoue-Labarthe, Philippe; *See also* Nancy, Jean-Luc
Poovey, Mary 4
poststructural
 -ism 2
 law of being social 124
 philosophy 42
 thought 2, 3, 5–6, 12–13, 78, 122
  of community 6
  of sociability 6
  of sociality 6

queer
 as exemple of infinite resistance 88
 being 78–81
 experience 76–9
 LGBT 78
 nation 79–80, 81, 85–6
 politics 77

Rousseau, Jean-Jacques 42
Rugo, Daniele 31

The Sense of the World. Nancy, Jean-Luc 47, 62, 67, 91–2
sociability. *See* poststructural: thought: of sociability; *See also* human nature; *See also* Hume, David; *See also* Kant, Immanuel: in Nancy; *See also* Nancy, Jean-Luc: ground(lessness) of being social; *See* law: of originary sociability
social contract. *See* Rousseau, Jean-Jacques
sociality. *See also* Hume, David; *See also* death: as basis of sociality; *See also* Butler: poetic sociality; *See also* poetry: as originary sociality
 as law 44

bare 122
contrasting notion of 7
evanesecence of 2
making sense of 93
normalized 4
of law 45
postructural reconfiguring of 2, 6
putting in question 11
renewed thinking of (in Nancy) 21, 29
unworked and trans-immanent 10
society 4, 33–8, 93
and law 38–46
civil 34, 35, 38
existential incoherence of 35
fictive 38
Gesellschaft 38
heteronormative 79, 86, 89
in Foucault 5, 33–4, 37
in Kant 19
in Nancy 7
occidental 38
taking on identity 40
socius 42, 115
standing man 72–5. *See also* Gezi Park protest
Stiegler, Bernard 11
subjectivity
imposed 104
legal 111
and poetry 104

The Truth of Democracy. Nancy, Jean-Luc 61
Taksim Square 72. *See also* standing man
Tataryn, Anatasia 13
Treatise on Human Nature. Hume, David 17–20

un-ground 25, 26
unworked community. *See also* Nancy, Jean-Luc: inoperative community

Wall, Illan rua 125, 127
Williams, Raymond 35, 38

www.ingramcontent.com/pod-product-compliance
Lightning Source LLC
Chambersburg PA
CBHW071351080526
44587CB00017B/3063